The Compassionate Activist

Lucy offers a unique perspective on compassionate activism drawn from her decades of living in Africa and working to help uphold and highlight the indigenous mindfulness traditions of the continent. Her work is authentic, heartfelt, and deeply beneficial.
Charlie Morley,
Bestselling Author of 'Dreaming through Darkness'

Lucy has the incredible gift of encouraging everyone around her to take the next daring step on their journey, both on and off the yoga mat or meditation cushion. She generously shares the wisdom and joy from her own practice and life experiences, and in this way, inspires others to follow their own path to growth. May this work bring possibility to many more aspiring movers and shakers in the world!
Steven Heyman
Yoga Works, South Africa

Lucy's bubbling enthusiasm for life in both its delightful and challenging aspects, infuses readers of her book with well-being and the resolve to live with gratitude. The Compassionate Activist is filled with simple, practical wisdom that makes for crystal-clear guidance and the development of personal insights. It is an easy-to-read workbook, with accessible stories illustrating the concepts described. May this lovely offering open hearts along the way.
Robyn Sheldon
Author of 'The Mama Bamba Way'
and 'The Liminal Lands'

A Journey Book:

The Compassionate Activist

Transforming the World
from Within

Lucy Draper-Clarke PhD

Portal Works

Published in South Africa by:
Portal Works

Copyright © Lucy Draper-Clarke, 2022

www.lucydraperclarke.com

The right of Lucy Draper-Clarke to be identified as the author of this work has been asserted by them in accordance with the Copyright, Designs and Patents Act 1988.

ISBN 978-0-6397-2341-9 (Paperback)

First Edition

Cover artwork and design by Andrea Rolfes, 2022
'The Compassionate Activist' by Emma Mary Mills, 2022
'The Dance of Creation' by Maxine Puren, 2020

Set in Adobe Caslon Pro 11/15pt
Printed and bound by Novus Print, South Africa

During the writing of this book, two spiritual leaders, whom I have long admired, passed away: Zen Master Thich Nhat Hanh and Archbishop Desmond Tutu.

They were both compassionate activists in the profoundest sense. Thich Nhat Hanh was a peace activist, who inspired the practice of Engaged Buddhism throughout the world. Archbishop Desmond Tutu, known as the Rabble-Rouser for Peace, played a vital role in South Africa's transition to democracy.

This book is dedicated to them, and to those who come after them: the leaders of the past, and the compassionate and engaged community who will lead us into the future.

Contents

Foreword by Rutendo Ngara — ix
Foreword by Warren Nebe — xi
Preface — xv

Introduction — 1
1. A Call to Stillness — 15
2. Circles of Safety — 34
3. Ways to Engage — 53
4. Our Indestructible Essence — 67
5. The Activist's Achilles — 80
6. The Activist Archetype — 101
7. Enlightened Self-Interest — 113
8. A Life of Purpose — 127
9. Resourcing and Self-Care — 139
10. Joy as Insurrection — 151
Moving Forward — 166

Appendices — 174
Acknowledgements — 180
References — 182
About the Author — 188

Foreword by Rutendo Ngara

Wholeness at a Time of Holeness

The year was 2020. Despite humanity's quests for 2020 vision through the age of modernity, clarity of seeing instead found the world wading through murky waters in a raging storm - blindfolded. 2020 was a time of unraveling.

At the hands of a microscopic sentient being, the COVID-19 virus, the world stopped in its tracks. Borders were closed, systems were shut down, economies catapulted into recession, health systems were strained, millions of sources of livelihood were lost and many of the prevailing ills of society were accentuated. The repetitive pleas of George Floyd, "I can't breathe!", as he was suffocated to death by a white policeman on 25 May 2020 reflected not only the modus operandi of the virus in restricting the body's respiratory system's ability to sustain life, but the constrictive nature of oppressive systems worldwide. "I can't breathe!" similarly spoke to the shifts in environmental factors as climate change becomes a startling reality.

The pandemic catapulted the world into pandemonium, unearthing the collective pathologies of humanity – seen only in the dilated pupils of society. Yet even as the virus mutates into normality, wars of differing shades and timbres rage on. In its intelligence, the virus has been a catalyzing force. In its belligerence, the virus has been an illuminator. In its resilience, the virus has been an activator. To Nigerian philosopher, Bayo Akomolafe, Coronavirus is at once a Mother, a Monster and an Activist. He tells us, "The times are urgent, so let us slow down."

During the throes of the chaos, a group of seasoned activists, scholars, artists, healers, visionaries and wisdom keepers began to gather in circle around the proverbial baobab tree, seeking to create new systems, foster new ways of working and build new paradigms for the future. In this, the Earthrise Collective braids the threads of Activism, Ancient Wisdom and Alternatives into a tapestry. As founding member of this Collective, Kabir Bavikatte, reflects, "The vision of Earthrise is one of Wholeness". This is a Wholeness that reminds us that we are 'a part' and not 'apart' from life. This Wholeness is relational, while allowing each individual to embody their own 'isnesses.' This Wholeness affords each node or knot a place in the cosmic web. This Wholeness is at once a crease in the fabric of Life… and the very fabric itself.

Yet this fabric is frayed at the edges. This crease has threads running bare. This vision is marred by the reality of "holeness". Holes in our thinking. Holes in our doing. Holes in our being. Isness has long given way to an 'othering' proclivity. Innovativeness has long stepped aside for dwindling creativity. An apartheid of ideas - a segregative propensity - has bound us in captivity. The dimming spark of life creates shadows seen only at the dusk of an epoch.

At this time of turning we seek a common passion; we seek engaged activity; we seek an alternative activism in our present, rooted in ancient wisdom, as a feedback loop to shepherd us into the arms of a benevolent future. This is a moment that calls out to the spirit of Sankofa. It is a moment screaming for Ntu – the original real reality, the source-force and the unified field that animates Ubuntu. It is a moment calling for both outer and inner revolution.

Lucy Draper-Clarke's work provides us such a bridge. The Compassionate Activist draws many tributaries from universal wisdoms, rooting us into the mutual duality of reality. Activism can foster meaningful engagement only if it takes time out to contemplate. It is in the stillness that action is born. It can only illuminate and shift the status quo when it delves into the shadows that merge into the night, eventually making way for the clarity of the day. In a time when inequality and lack of equity abounds, activism calls us into the realms of equanimity. We slow down into the urgency. Trans-formation, re-storation and re-generation, can only begin from within.

This work- and play-book gives us new tools to create alternative fabrics of reality. It gives us new threads to weave fresh tapestries of creativity. It gives us new imaginaries to manifest emergent fractals of activity. It brings a 2020 vision of wholeness into a time of holeness.

Rutendo L Ngara - healer, philosopher and engineer

Foreword by Warren Nebe

In a time of profound hurt. In a time when people are walking wounded. In a time of local, national, and global catastrophe, Lucy Draper-Clarke's *The Compassionate Activist* opens a door for us to bridge an old world order; one that will surely see our demise as a human species if we do not evolve into a conscious, compassionate, and responsive world to address the urgent crises we face.

The Compassionate Activist is born in a country that is the most unequal in the world. South Africa is plagued by a legacy of Colonialism, Apartheid, and corruption, in a context of crippling global inequality, as witnessed by the COVID-19 pandemic, where unemployment, substance use, and violence are epidemics. The country's public discourse has been hijacked by international and local economic and reactionary forces that propel dialogue into binaries, minimising complexity and nuance, creating alternate narratives devoid of reality, and rendering it difficult to usher in critical change through informed, meaningful conversation and action. These challenges are by no means unique to South Africa.

My work with young people studying to become facilitators of social change constantly reveals that they are attuned to the complex reality they find themselves in, and understand significantly the crises humanity faces. Still, they all too often express overwhelm and hopelessness. The greater the national and global crises, the more they turn inward, focusing on the domestic or personal realms. In this space of the individual, an area limited in context, young people are becoming psychologically entangled, losing significant social relationships, and battling mental health demons that are often the business of a public health emergency and not a private affair. This implosion of self in the world sorely needs agency, voice, and social engagement as its medicine. Our desire may be for the old world order that has produced the climate emergency to implode, but we certainly don't want our children and youth to implode. This is no answer for finding our way into the future. So, how do we begin to map routes for ourselves, young and old, to become the change we urgently seek?

I recently worked with a large team of professional facilitators for gender-based violence (GBV) prevention for a mining company and its surrounding communities in a remote, arid region in South Africa. Over three months, we engaged with peoples' stories about micro and macro gender-based aggressions, stories of traumatic memory, and stories that spoke to the present unspeakable crisis. Our purpose was to listen to diverse peoples' stories from all sectors and levels of the workplace, within the mines and communities, to witness those stories and reflect them back to those who had the courage to tell them publicly. GBV is a complex matter. It requires a depth of engagement that goes to the heart of what social change requires. A challenge arises when the problem is of epidemic proportions, just like in a war context, where everyone is implicitly or explicitly implicated. Our job is to activate and unravel the stories of violence enacted through the politics of gender; to name the problem so we can understand what it is we need to address; and to find ways to keep people listening and engaged.

Early on in the process, I needed to reflect personally on how I was showing up. Here I was, inviting stories about violence into the public space, no matter who the teller was and what the content was, with the promise that I could hold, witness, and reflect them back, without judgement. On the one hand, I was entering the space as an activist seeking to unearth the causes of the triggers of violence, whether large or small. My position was clear. We needed to fight this scourge in our society. On the other hand, I needed to be a compassionate witness the storytelling to elicit a public understanding of the violence. It was, in this instance, a moment of spiritual reckoning. Not only did I need to reflect on how GBV has permeated my life, but I also had to revisit the permeable relationship between victim and perpetrator. In this, I was guided by my training, professional experience, and approach. Alice Walker's work served as a guiding force. The cyclical nature of the abuser and abused when trauma remains buried and unconscious is at the heart of this work. But, still. This was not enough to give me the grounding, integrity, and authenticity I was personally looking for.

What did I need to do to face a group of people with integrity? What did I need to do to be present, to listen, and to hold space without judgement, fear, or unconscious punitive nuances indicated in the eye, head, hand movement, or verbal utterance? How could I be compassionate in my presence?

In a moment, standing before white Afrikaans men whom I'd grown up fearing because of the historical, cultural, and political violence; meeting the eyes of Black men and women who distrust men like me with white skins; facing men who fear and hate Queer men like me; being repulsed by those who clearly don't believe GBV is a problem; and looking at women and men who hold painful, anguish-filled stories, I meditated. If I love myself enough, I said to myself, I can love you.

In that moment, I could stand separate, firmly rooted on the ground, present to who was in the room, and open to receive their stories. All of their stories. I could be the activist helping to unearth the individual, social, and systemic stories of trauma, and I could be the compassionate witness who hears the stories of psychological, social, and professional cycles of abuse. Being compassionate with myself, with all of who I am, allowed me to not lose myself in the overwhelm of trauma and stress embedded in each and every story. bell hooks' legacy of transformative love was my teacher here. Being compassionate allowed me to be separate, but connected with every storyteller. It sustained my ability to keep showing up as a compassionate activist. Sustainable change in a time of unprecedented crises that emerged from love.

It is here that Lucy's *The Compassionate Activist* offers a significant way forward for our work in education, development, therapy, and activism. Drawing on her own rich experience that cuts across three continents, carefully bridging Western traditions of learning and science with Eastern traditions of spirituality, and landing in Southern Africa, Lucy manages to lucidly navigate and integrate pathways for becoming a transformative activist in the 21st century.

This book is a powerful road map for seasoned and young activists worldwide. And here, I speak of activists as our future leaders, teachers, economists, therapists, artists, social workers, farmers, and climate change and sustainable environmental practitioners. It is a deeply felt and gentle evocation for all of us to take stock of our internal resources, attitudes, and assumptions about activism, guiding us to explore what will sustain us in becoming genuinely compassionate in, and through, our activism.

Above all, and importantly, it offers hope in a time of many and immense challenges.

Warren Nebe, Founder, Drama for Life, University of the Witwatersrand

Preface

In December 2004, I embarked on a dream holiday. Flying from Botswana to Thailand, I was bound for a yoga retreat on an island paradise. Although I arrived alone, the yoga practice opened hearts and minds, forging lasting friendships.

A few days after I'd left the yoga centre, shocking headlines dominated the news, accompanied by devastating images of the tsunami that had wiped out large areas of Asia, including the yoga centre where I had stayed. Within a week, I was back on the coast of Thailand, working alongside the retreat manager, Bodhi Garrett, the Thai staff, and the overseas volunteers, to set up the North Andaman Tsunami Relief organisation.

It was a time of great sorrow, as we witnessed peoples' losses, again and again. Entire villages had been washed into the sea. We cried together at the suffering of the tsunami victims and their families. Yet we also connected, played and laughed, drawing great meaning from the work. Joy somehow seemed to co-exist with our sorrow; the fellowship of people working together with a shared intention. I took on the role of storyteller, communicating with overseas donors to develop a sense of solidarity, and accompanying Thai village residents as they worked to rebuild their lives.

Without feeling the depths of sadness, I'm not sure we could ever have appreciated the bubbling moments of delight; of helping to plan and rebuild houses, schools, and businesses. We witnessed people making conscious choices as to how to navigate their lives going forward. These sights, stories, and experiences somehow turned the disaster into an opportunity for development. Joy and sorrow were the warp and weft that weaved together a consoling blanket of humanity. It was a deeply inspiring year, during which I was able to learn that running an organisation from ethical principles could give enormous power and reach to our efforts.

Disaster relief is a specific type of activism. The world was on our side, sending money so that we could support the communities to develop in whichever ways they chose. It was a year of magic and manifesting; whatever project we were asked to develop, or support, seemed to come into being almost spontaneously.

Fast forward five years, and I found myself in Johannesburg, setting out on the path of a PhD at the University of the Witwatersrand, an institution known for its commitment to the end of apartheid. I was conducting research on mindfulness in education, as my own experiences had revealed its powerful impact on me, my relationships, and my work.

I wanted to see whether the student teachers who learnt these practices, could find meaning, joy, and compassion, in their classrooms, and inspire a new generation of learners. What I actually found was story after story of suffering: a student thrown out of his accommodation by the Red Ants (an eviction company), stories of hijackings and break-ins, tales of families divided, and the pressures placed on first generation black African students whose families were depending on them to study, work and send money home.

The results of the Depression Anxiety Stress Scale that I administered were higher than for clinical populations in other countries, yet these were students going into schools; students from whom we expected compassion and care – qualities that they so rarely received or experienced themselves.

I was overwhelmed by the enormity of the problems in the Education sector, and when I started connecting with other educators and changemakers, I could feel that sense of despair and exhaustion, even cynicism, from all sectors – social entrepreneurs, human rights' advocates, and climate justice activists. It seemed that the promise of the Rainbow Nation had lost its brilliance, and everything was turning grey. The political transformation of the '90s had not been matched by social and economic transformation, and a sense of despondency and bitterness was palpable.

I started wondering how I could navigate these dual experiences – the inspiration, joy, and social cohesion, in Thailand, and the polarisation, and sense of overwhelm, in South Africa. Over time, it became clear that I wanted to share how to keep touching into joy with others, even in the midst of sorrow. To this end, I've since been exploring how contemplative practices can inform the work of changemakers and activists.

I believe that compassionate activism is about cultivating an ethic of care and engagement, bringing people together to address humanity's many challenges. This relationship with the world is accessible to more than just those who might identify with the identity and term of 'activist'.

I believe it offers an expansive and inclusive approach to staying involved with the world around us, based on the willingness to focus on change within ourselves.

Compassionate activism is for everyone; we can all bring joy and compassion to the world around us.

Pic 1. The Compassionate Activist, by Emma Mary Mills

Introduction

*"Yesterday I was clever;
so I wanted to change the world,
Today I am wise; so I am changing myself."*
~ *Rumi*

Rumi's words ring so true when I look at the trajectory of my own life. At university in England, my friends and I would spend hours discussing how to end global disparities and north-south divides. We were horrified by the apartheid system in South Africa, and the power of multinational companies to hold developing world countries to ransom. We wrote assignments about the movement of capital around the world, and the cycles of boom and bust that left so many human and environmental casualties.

It was the late 1980s, and we already knew about climate change, unable to understand why no-one was doing anything. We'd take part in heated arguments, assuming everyone who did not agree with us was stupid, rather than trying to take the time to understand their point of view. We rarely discussed our own privilege, and the way of life we took for granted. Our focus was outward, not inward.

I started writing this book before the COVID-19 pandemic in an attempt to answer the question: "What can we do, in our individual and collective lives, to create a shift to a more inclusive, cohesive, and life-sustaining world?"

The need seems greater now. We've become deeply aware of our interconnectedness, with other people, and with our natural world. We've also become aware of our human frailty, and the impact of isolation on our mental health. So many people have experienced deep suffering, and even more have shown their extraordinary capacity for care. The pandemic laid bare the pervasive and persistent nature of oppressive structures such as racism and sexism. I often get disillusioned that this structural oppression so severely limits the potential of the global majority, and I have to find ways to remind myself that when we transform as individuals, and come together in solidarity with others, structures can change, too.

The compassionate actions of individuals and communities have helped us to navigate this time of groundlessness. We may once have thought that our lives followed a predictable pattern, but the pandemic revealed how little control we truly have.

So, what can we do amidst overwhelming uncertainty?

We can attend to what is within, and around, us moment-to-moment. And we must also keep in mind the societal norms and structures that support, or diminish, this personal agency.

I've been heartened by the work of Erica Chenoweth, an American political scientist and professor of public policy at the Harvard Kennedy School and the Radcliffe Institute for Advanced Study, which reveals that only 3.5% of a population needs to be involved in peaceful protests for political change to take place. It is my hope that the contents of this book serve as one more inspiration to access that tipping point into a caring and regenerative future.

Within these pages, I highlight the need for inner transformation, and the willingness to address the structural and global issues that harm so many living beings. I reflect on how to support the suffering of others, from an ethic of care, without getting mired in anger or sorrow, through the inclusion of both contemplative practices and practical actions.

This is activism as a relational practice, rather than activism as conflict. It is engagement inspired by love, not hate. It is mobilisation through the gathering of people, not blasting them apart. It is feeding, not fighting, because we need to feed ourselves, while we feed those around us.

The practices I share are drawn from the places I have lived, and the inspiring people I have met along the way. Although English by nationality, I was born in Sri Lanka and educated in the United Kingdom, before settling in Botswana and South Africa.

My feet are grounded in the Eastern wisdom traditions, particularly Buddhism. My head has been influenced by a Western style of education, and I'm fascinated by contemplative neuroscience and evolutionary psychology. More recently, and most importantly, my heart has expanded through the joys and sorrows of life in Africa. This is where I've learnt about the importance of community, and the relational philosophy of Ubuntu. My inner questions have shifted from, "Who am I?" to "How can I live well, in relationship with others?"

Admittedly, it's been hard to know when to stop writing, as I shift, and change, and engage, with the world in different ways. But at a certain point, I must draw a line, and set my ideas free to be tried and tested, and then improved upon by others. I offer this book onwards, with the deep wish that it evolves and grows as required by our world, and the beings that live within it. I sense that we have moved into a new time; time to transform the world from the inside out, and transform ourselves from the outside in.

Readers of this Book

My intention is to offer support to all changemakers, wherever you feel called to make an impact. You may be an extroverted activist, energised by being out in the world, getting things done, and working in social or climate justice arenas. Alternatively, you may be more introverted, drawn to the contemplative, creative, or academic side; sitting alone or in nature, focusing quietly on your family and community, while creating knowledge or art. Every now and again, you may find yourself being called upon, perhaps unwillingly, to engage.

Whatever role you play, we all need the support of others. I've witnessed too many wonderful, passionate, and open-hearted people burn out. They become cynical and overwhelmed by the fear of what life might be like for their children, and the never-ending challenges to humanity.

I've also met many meditators and spiritual practitioners who know that inner transformation is necessary, as it's where we have the most ability to affect change. Yet sometimes, they extract themselves from the world, believing that they are not wise enough or compassionate enough to engage with social and climate justice issues. My suggestion is to make our relationship with the material world into a distinct aspect of our spiritual practice. It can be a powerful place to put compassion into action. You may never feel that you're transformed enough to act with pure, altruistic intention, yet it is through the engagement itself that you can monitor your spiritual development and see where transformation is still required.

Wherever you fall on this contemplative-activist spectrum, it is useful to note that our combined skills can be of enormous benefit to society. It's time to work in solidarity with others, and not on our own. We need to harness the qualities and talents of everyone. Van Jones, an African American changemaker, describes this potential:

> *"The convergence of spiritual people becoming active, and activist people becoming spiritual, creates a lot of possibility for real change. It's very difficult to make change externally if we are not emotionally healthy enough to get through conflict. We need 360 degrees of change inside and out, to survive as a species."*
> *Van Jones*

Underpinning Theories

The ideas in this book have been informed by my interest, research, and practice in three different fields: Mahayana and Vajrayana Buddhism, Contemplative Science, and Evolutionary Psychology. My Buddhist teachers have been hugely influential in my life, offering a vast range of meditation techniques to address all situations, as well as to focus me on the bodhicitta motivation to help all beings.

Contemplative Science, particularly neuroscience, has provided the proof of what meditators have long been aware of – that training the mind can change the physical structure and neural pathways in the brain. Additionally, my readings of Evolutionary Psychology have provided me with an understanding both of why we have such an incredible capacity for love, and our shadow side, where hate and aggression reside. It shows the full spectrum of human capability and affirms why training in compassion can support our on-going evolution of consciousness.

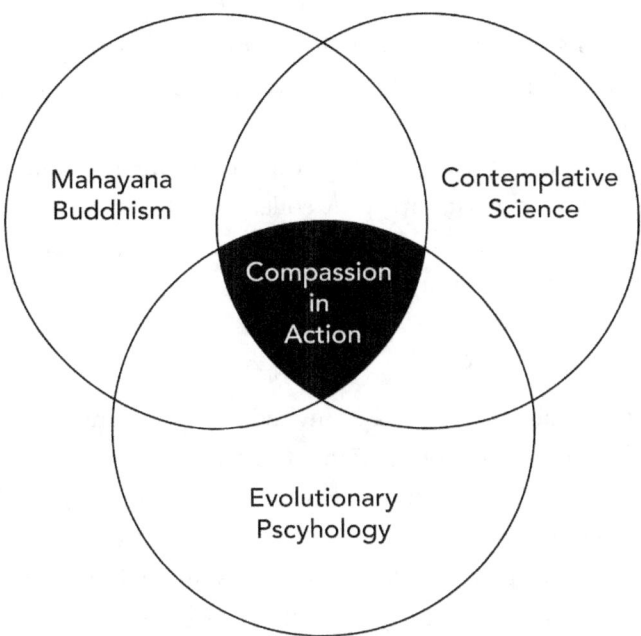

Fig 1. Underpinning Theories

We need to move beyond affiliation only for family, and like-minded social groups, to affiliation with all beings – human, animal, and the planet itself. And it's worth asking, if we viewed the natural world as a living being, like you or me, would we still treat it as badly as we do?

How to Use this Book

The structure of this book is a 10-week course that combines theory, stories, and home practices, and you can work through it as a self-study guide, keeping a journal record of the practices, and your insights. It can also be helpful to work through it with a friend, or an accountability partner, week-by-week.

For those who find it supportive, you may opt to have a facilitator as you progress through the pages; someone who holds the space each week for meditation and discussion. This can also be in a peer-led group where you rotate the facilitation role.

Learning to step into a leadership role is important, as is learning to step back and be led by others. It all forms part of the reflective practice required by this work. I strongly feel that this process lends itself to a peer-supported approach, as a way to acknowledge each other's incredible potential for creativity and altruism, while also caring for each other's shadow side.

If you are doing the course within your organisation, you might first need to develop trust with your colleagues. To assist with this, I give guidelines for running weekly sessions at the end of the book (in Appendix A, entitled Cultivating Trust).

Foundational Practices

In each chapter, you'll be invited to experiment with several practices that form the foundation of Compassionate Activism. These are 1) Contemplative practices, 2) Engagement practices, and 3) Shadow Integration practices.

Some of these practices ask you to turn inwards, while others encourage an outward turn, so that you engage with the people and the world around you. Shadow Integration practices invite you to face what you find difficult; an act that can take significant courage, supported by self-compassion.

You may already be familiar with many types of Contemplative practice, but it can be useful to list them. Let's divide them into three categories: a) Calming practices, b) Insight practices, and c) Practices to cultivate positive qualities. Each of these helps strengthen the other, but it's not a linear path. Rather, it more closely resembles an ever-expanding spiral.

Calming meditations use a specific point of focus on which to concentrate, such as the body, the breath, or the senses. These have helped me personally to train my mind to stay present, despite external distractions. Once I'm able to achieve a basic level of calm, I find that it's easier to open my mind to the experiences that move through moment-by-moment. I can then gain insight into how my habit patterns run the show, until I can identify them clearly. These are usually habits from times in childhood when I had fewer resources or means with which to cope with life's challenges. Once I notice them and acknowledge that these habits were once skilful responses to difficult circumstances, they transform or sometimes, even disappear.

Through these practices of calming and insight, we begin to live with a greater sense of contentment and ease. We also experience greater harmony with others, and when there is disharmony, it becomes easier to identify the cause by looking within ourselves, rather than attributing blame externally.

In terms of cultivating our innate positive qualities, the practices will allow us to look to the virtues described in all spiritual traditions, such as love, kindness, gratitude, generosity, and compassion. Compassion is at the heart of our approach to activism, and there are two types of compassion: aspirational compassion, and compassion in action. First, we must aspire to develop the capacity for compassion. We do this quietly, at home, using the ancient practices that have supported meditators for generations. Then we put this capacity into action, ensuring that it lives beyond us and beyond our own lifespan.

By developing the aspiration to help others, we're able to expand our circle wider through experimentation with Engagement practices. They offer a method of gaining insight into our intentions and habit patterns, both the helpful and the harmful ones. And in light of this, we're soon able to see whether our intentions are self-centred or genuinely altruistic. If we can engage, without craving for appreciation or reward, we're moving in the right direction! We're slowly finding our way towards equanimity, where we can hold ourselves steady in the face of suffering and be of great benefit to the world around us. I explore a variety of different ways to engage in this book, from helping a friend to participating in collective action.

Personally, I think of Shadow Integration practices as the bridge between contemplation and engagement. When we engage, and difficult emotions arise or things go wrong, it is usually a sign that something within us needs to be taken care of. The shadow aspects of our mind still need to be integrated. When we have the courage to turn and face our own shadow, we can transform our disturbing emotions and tendencies into powerful insights and wisdom. By facing injustice from a place of clear-seeing and compassion-based engagement, we avoid the tendency to perpetuate the same problems through our own behaviour. And this requires the uncomfortable realisation that we're often complicit in the difficulties we see in the world around us.

Slowly, with the support of these practices, I've begun to experience longer-term, bottom-up changes within myself. I'm not triggered quite as often by external circumstances. However, there remains much work to be done – and in this, it seems like I'm not alone. There are many ancient stories of meditators who spend years in a cave, only to walk back into daily life, and start arguing with their family members. They swiftly return to the cave for some more years of meditation!

The table on Contemplative, Engagement and Shadow Integration Practices is one way of categorising the techniques you'll find in this book. It offers a brief description of each practice and its benefits. Audio versions of the contemplative practices offered in the chapters are also available for download from my website (www.lucydraperclarke.com).

You may be familiar with other practices from your own spiritual or religious tradition. There is no 'best type' of meditation, as it needs to be adapted to your personality, and your moment-by-moment needs. Because of this, it's ideal to work with a teacher or spiritual director who can offer support and suggestions. You can also find your own way initially, with friends and mediation apps, until you build up the confidence in your capacity to find balance.

Contemplative, Engagement and Shadow Integration Practices

1. CONTEMPLATIVE PRACTICES		
a) CALMING PRACTICES		
Practice	Description	Benefits
Moving Body-Based Practices	Yoga, qi gong, tai chi, walking meditation, running, dance, drumming	Improves interoception, cultivates awareness of the embodied mind, calms the nervous system, and releases trauma
Supine Body-Based Practices	Body-scan, yoga nidra, muscle relaxation	Shifts into the parasympathetic nervous response, soothing.
Breathwork Practices	Pranayama, abdominal breath, activating, balancing, and calming breath practices	Soothes, balances, and energises, while shifting into parasympathetic nervous response
Focused Attention (Mindfulness Support)	Concentrating on a chosen object e.g. breath, sound, a candle, a mantra, or chanting	A peaceful, yet alert state of mind, a concentrated mind, focused on the present moment
Prayer	Connecting with a higher power and asking for guidance	Gives rise to a feeling of connection and support

b) INSIGHT PRACTICES		
Practice	Description	Benefits
Open Monitoring	Witnessing moment-by-moment changes in experience and noticing habits of the mind	Non-reactive monitoring, non-judgment, identifying our unique pathways of habit
Reflection	Dropping questions into a calm mind	Deep listening to inner, embodied wisdom
Contemplation	Focusing on a text or guiding concepts	Learning from the wisdom of others

c) CULTIVATING POSITIVE QUALITIES		
Practice	Description	Benefits
Gratitude	Using a daily journal, or a letter to another	Eases depression, shifts focus away from toxic emotions
Loving-Kindness	Sending out well-wishes to self, others, difficult people, and all living beings in ever-widening circles	Cultivation of kindness with consequent experience of joy
Self-Compassion	Focusing on mindfulness, common humanity, and self-kindness at times of difficulty	Builds resilience, reduces rumination, overcomes difficulties
Compassion	Tonglen – giving and taking on the breath	Builds compassionate motivation and resilience
Forgiveness	Releasing the constriction between self and another	Distinguishes between the person who causes harm and their actions; reduces our own suffering

Visualisation	Bringing an image of an inspiring person or place into the mind	Uses the creative aspect of the mind for self-regulation and personal transformation

2. ENGAGEMENT PRACTICES

Practice	Description	Benefits
Change for Change	Offering small change to those in need	Always having something to give
Supporting a Friend	Offering practical and emotional help and care	Learning equanimity – being equally open to appreciation or rejection.
Donating a Meal	Giving up a meal and offering the money equivalent to a soup kitchen or charity	Fasting helps shift focus from self to other; donating overcomes greed
Tithing	Offering 10% of your income or time	Experiencing the benefits of the two directional flow of giving and receiving
Collective Action	Bringing people together around an issue	Learning that 'I can't, but we can'
Nonviolent Direct Action	Public gatherings to express objection or dissent towards an idea or action, or to propose alternatives	Demonstrates solidarity with those negatively affected; opportunity for creative interventions that move people emotionally.

3. SHADOW INTEGRATION PRACTICES		
Practice	Description	Benefits
Noticing Disturbing Emotions and Triggers	Bringing awareness to the rejected aspects of the psyche	Identifying both the dark and golden shadow, allowing integration of the psyche, learning to feel without reactivity
Exploring and Understanding Disturbing Emotions	Identifying when difficult emotions arise and understanding their evolutionary necessity	Choosing what to water and what to weed out
Transforming Disturbing Emotions	Using non-violent communication to engage with situations when difficult emotions arise	Expressing our feelings and needs, without triggering others

Relationship with the Practices

You may feel a sense of safety and connection when doing some of the practices, while others can bring up huge resistance. There may be many that feel neither pleasant, nor unpleasant. When I first started to meditate, yoga and qi gong really helped regulate my breath and prepare my body for the sitting practices. Only after movement could I quieten down and focus. In contrast, when I was introduced to walking meditation, I felt really irritated. My relationship with walking was about reaching a destination, and getting there fast. The slow, mindful steps felt pointless and frustrating. My reactivity pointed clearly to my preference for product over process, and pace over patience. Having observed my relationship with walking meditation change over the years, I've also been able to witness my inner world shift slightly.

Pay attention to the practices that feel supportive for you, as they help to sustain you on this long road of personal transformation. Equally, bring curiosity to the practices you resist, the ones that feel tight and uncomfortable. The easier ones are very important for downregulating your nervous system so that you can respond, rather than react, to life's obstacles. Those that challenge you will point towards your internal places of resistance. They are asking to be integrated and transformed.

Learning self-compassion felt like a huge weight of judgement had been taken off my shoulders. I was so relieved that I was allowed to be a flawed human being and to adapt my practice to suit the way I was feeling during each meditation session.

Often, we can default to a familiar meditation practice, even if it would be more beneficial to use a technique that provides the antidote to our state of mind. For example, if you are feeling distracted and scattered, a calming, focused attention practice might help re-centre you. Or if you are experiencing sadness or difficulty, a self-compassion practice can be the most effective way to take care of your needs, or an engagement practice that shifts your focus from yourself to others.

To live fully is to experience the full range of human emotion. We learn to respect the information our body and heart provide and use those impulses to know when action is required. Controlling your emotions in public may be more socially acceptable, but we are allowed to feel, and a daily meditation practice gives us the chance to do this.

Different practices produce different results, and many of the ancient meditation practices, taught for over two thousand years, have recently been investigated through neuroscience research. Studies, on gratitude for example, have revealed what meditators have long been aware of through their own experience: meditating changes the way we view and respond to the world.

One way of gauging the fruits of our practice is when those close to us start to comment that our habit patterns are changing because they often notice, sooner than we do. I remember hearing a lovely story about a mother with a young family. She was being pulled in so many directions that she was feeling overwhelmed. After finding a meditation course, she carried out her daily practice diligently. She would take herself off to her room and meditate quietly. Of course, her children didn't like it. When she was practicing, they would suddenly call for water, or snacks, or help with something. However, she persevered, telling them that she needed some quiet time and would attend to their needs as soon as she was done. After several weeks, the course ended, the school holidays came, and she had an influx of visitors. With so many people needing her care and attention, she found that she could not prioritise her daily practice. She let it slip, not noticing initially the differences in her method of coping with external demands. It was then that she overheard the children talking about her; the same children who had resented her practice initially. Her son was saying, "I wish Mummy would go back into her room and do that thing again. She is so much nicer to us when she is doing it every day!"

We don't easily notice the change in ourselves when we are doing practice because our inner world still feels chaotic, and we are constantly distracted by thoughts. However, as we learn to be aware of thoughts and feelings, and can respond to them with gentle acceptance, other people can pick up on these qualities, and feel safer in our presence. When people feel drawn to us, then it is easy to bring a community together around a specific issue. This is where the meditator can become a changemaker.

Most of the practices in this book are simple, but this doesn't mean that they're easy. It is helpful to practice in a group, so that you have support as you move along this challenging path of self-awareness. It is worth it, though, so don't give up. The more freedom we feel within ourselves, the greater support we can be to the people and world around us.

CHAPTER 1
A Call to Stillness

"Only when it is dark enough can you see the stars."
~ Martin Luther King Jnr

We're facing several concurrent crises - the climate crisis, mental and physical health crises, and a crisis of consciousness. Communities are increasingly polarised, and people are becoming more isolated and more lonely, despite our technological connectivity. We seem to have lost touch with the fundamental truths of interconnectedness and reciprocity.

How are you feeling about the state of our world? I find myself fluctuating between hope and despair, joy and sorrow, often accompanied by overwhelm or even anger. With the news we see on our devices, it's easy to get overwhelmed, to feel that nothing can be done to shift the direction in which the world is headed. Given the States of Emergency we've created, I often notice a contraction in my body, and the energy leaching out of me. I struggle to find the words to express what I'm experiencing and feel the urge to close off and hide or find someone else to blame. But why is this?

When we experience times of difficulty, we tend to respond in one of two ways: hyper-arousal or hypo-arousal. Activists largely tend towards the former, and get 'stuck on', always needing to fix and change the situation in front of them, without necessarily being able to identify the underlying cause. This is hyper-arousal. Alternatively, we can also get overwhelmed and move into hypo-arousal, where we get 'stuck off', and feel like there is nothing that can be done. Both approaches have negative repercussions for us, as individuals, and for the people around us, and the systems in which we're embedded.

Neuroscience research has revealed that humans have complex brains, which are broadly divided into three parts. One part, the brainstem, focuses on survival. Another, the limbic system, is linked to emotions and our need for social connection. The third, the prefrontal cortex, controls intellectual functioning, language, and self-awareness.

When we experience, or just read about, frightening events, our brain defaults to the survival instinct. Fear and anxiety impair our immune system, organ health, and brain function. We find ourselves triggered, sometimes physically ill, and unable to access our creative capacities. It is this reactive survival mind that can send us down the pathway of despair, unless we can train it to stay focused on the reality of life in front of our own eyes.

Restoring the Balance

There is a beautiful Tibetan word, sowa, which means healing difficulties from the past, and creating the conditions for future health and wholeness. Taking care of our childhood wounds through therapeutic practices, and then learning how to work skilfully with our emotions, means we do not pass on trauma to the next generation. In recent years, trauma specialists such as Deb Dana have started using the terminology of the Window of Presence or Tolerance (Figure 2), which refers to the healthy functioning of our nervous system. It is the place of emotional and mental balance.

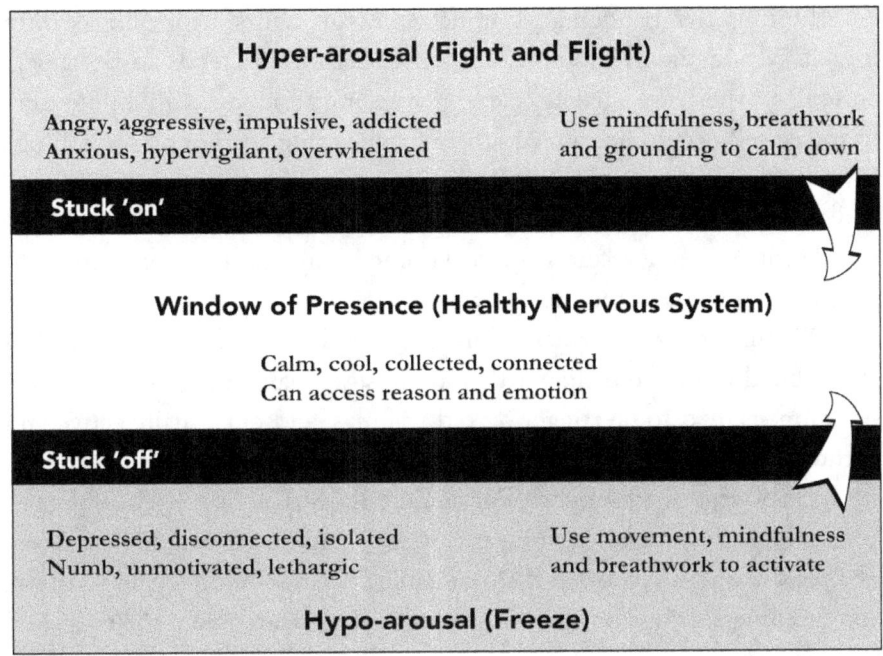

Fig 2. The Window of Presence

This model, summarised in Figure 2, suggests the ways we can regulate our states of hyper- and hypo-arousal, so that our brain and body are capable of functioning optimally, to keep us safe and allow us to find creative solutions to challenges. It has brought the practices of mindfulness meditation, breathwork, and mindful movement to the forefront of trauma work.

Contemplative Practice: Mindfulness

Bring your feet onto the earth and your sitz bones onto the chair or cushion. Feel these points of contact and allow them to ground you. Now, notice the passage of breath in and out of your nostrils. Allow the inbreath to expand your belly, your ribs, your chest. Then feel the sensation as you breathe out again. Can you relax a little? Continue with three more conscious breaths and take note of whether you feel a little more centred afterwards. This is sometimes all a mindfulness practice needs to be. It is an invitation to become a little more grounded and centred in the present moment.

During the pandemic, I noticed certain shifts happening within myself. My instinctive response, when I feel unsafe, tends to be hyper-arousal. I experience anxiety and anger, racing thoughts, and a pounding heart, as well as chronic pain and the overwhelming need to 'do something'. Over the course of a year, this shifted to a state of hypo-arousal; a numbness and shutting down, a sense of emptiness and withdrawal. I felt I was losing my identity and as a result, I stopped doing many of the things that I love, such as yoga and community work.

My university colleagues in Johannesburg noticed similar shifts within our applied drama and drama therapy postgraduate students. The global situation seemed to be triggering old traumas, and our usually active and enthusiastic students were becoming depressed, lethargic, and unable to study. They requested support. For communities that have been subject to generations of oppression, intergenerational trauma is carried in the body. The pandemic set in motion the trauma responses of brain fog, exhaustion, and numbness. It was healing for the students to learn about the roots and triggers of these responses, and we offered them self-care practices.

After noticing this shift and withdrawal within myself, my balancing response was to move. I made a commitment to dance every day, and took part in an online dance training, called Expressive Movement. It was a beautiful means of combining the receptivity and presence of a mindfulness practice, with the creativity and connection of moving in community (albeit online) and I began to take note of how each quality of a meditative life - silence, stillness, and solitude - had a more active counterpart. Sound balanced out silence, movement allowed me to appreciate stillness, and community took the loneliness out of solitude. These restoring practices are what brought me back to life, and back to the completion of this book.

My personal experience mirrored the experiences of others, inspiring my colleagues to develop and test a Healing Arts Pedagogy, which uses arts-based practices to un-cramp trauma from the body. We offered them to our students online, including rhythmic movement, breathwork, storytelling, and dance, and we all felt the sense of being led back to the shamanic practices of our forebears, who would gather around a fire and dance themselves back to health in community.

> *"In many shamanic societies, if you came to a medicine person*
> *complaining of being disheartened, dispirited, or depressed,*
> *they would ask one of four questions:*
> *When did you stop dancing?*
> *When did you stop singing?*
> *When did you stop being enchanted by stories?*
> *When did you stop being comforted by*
> *the sweet territory of silence?"*
> *~ Gabrielle Roth*

Being and Doing

It can be useful to distinguish between our two modes of mind – the being and doing modes; the contemplation and the engagement. Doing mode is very useful for attending to daily life tasks and meeting specific goals, but it doesn't help us cope with worries, or with events outside our control, such as uncertainty about the future or the things others are doing. When we try to apply doing mode to such situations, it can drain us mentally and leave us feeling stressed and overwhelmed.

In light of this, it's important to train your mind to spend more time in the present moment; in the Being mode. Being mode involves paying attention to your experiences without judging them or trying to change them. There is a sense of freedom and curiosity, and we can even start to see how the future emerges from the multidimensional complexity of the present moment. The irony is that the Being mode is a creative mode of mind, which can allow us to solve the problems that our Doing mode has brought about. You may be familiar with the quote attributed to Albert Einstein: "A problem cannot be solved at the same level of thinking that created it."

The collective actions we take in the next few years will determine whether the earth is able to sustain human life for the generations to come. The question worth asking is whether this could be the chance for us all to pull together and for everyone to use their unique skills to benefit the collective? If we do not, we risk continuing down the pathway of self-centredness, and destruction of the planet on which our very lives depend. This feels like an important moment for both personal and social transformation; a time to birth a global society that is socially just and ecologically regenerative.

But how can we do that?

It was in an attempt to sustain myself that I started exploring ideas and practices around Compassionate Activism, drawn from the ancient wisdom traditions of the global South and the East, as well as Western psychology and neuroscience. The research has helped to open my eyes to the millions of people who work quietly within their communities, supporting those who need help. These quiet activists find purpose and contentment through being in service to others. They rarely draw attention to what they do, simply meeting each moment as it presents itself.

These are the ordinary people who feel compelled to act on an issue close to their hearts, without any expectation of a quick result. They are the pebble in the pond that can create far-reaching ripples of change. Collective action always starts locally, yet it has the power to spread far and wide if it is addressing something that's felt by many. We never know when such shifts will happen, such moments of pebble-initiated change, but when they do, transformation can be swift. For example, few of us could have predicted that amidst a pandemic, the #BlackLivesMatter movement, initiated by grieving families several years before, would suddenly become a call for racial justice resounding all over the world.

Often the most committed changemakers are those whose experience of trauma or suffering awaken a life-long passion to ensure that others do not suffer the same things. Being wounded can prove powerful motivation, but it also has a shadow side that we need to acknowledge by exploring ways to transform it into wise action.

Of course, this doesn't apply to everyone. Some changemakers may have experienced a safe and happy childhood, becoming aware at some point of the suffering of others through their capacity for empathy and sense of interconnectedness. The differing entries to action make the worth of the changemaker's endeavours no less necessary or valuable.

The call to stillness and silence is as important as the call to action. This enhanced receptivity allows us to see deeply into the causes of our current situation. Contemplative practices play a vital role in helping us shift from survival to sanity, and the opportunity to awaken our full potential. We know instinctively that if enough people come together around an issue, motivated by the common good, we can reach a tipping point, and shifts happens.

This has happened many times before. South Africa offers a noteworthy example of such radical social and political change, which led to the end of apartheid. However, the country has not been immune from the shadow that unconsciously drives us towards self-interest, at the expense of others. If we do not transform our individual and collective consciousness, as we work towards restorative justice, then we may find ourselves perpetuating the systems that hold inequality in place.

Cultivating Awareness

Nomfundo Mogapi, a clinical psychologist with the Centre for the Study of Violence and Reconciliation in South Africa, studies the psychosocial healing of individuals, institutions, and collectives. In her research, she asks how we can carry out effective community development if those who want to do the work are broken and depleted; if those in positions of leadership are wounded and exhausted; and if the institutions that are vehicles for carrying out the work are dysfunctional.

She differentiates between individuals who carry their history of trauma into their work, and those who've healed their wounds to carry peace into the communities around them (Figure 3).

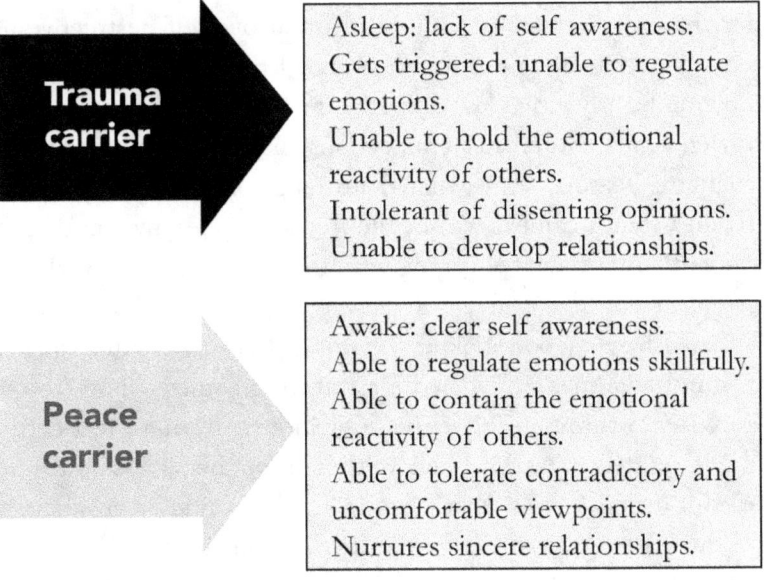

Fig 3. Trauma and Peace Carriers

She asks whether we are willing to do the inner work that will shift us from trauma-carriers to peace-carriers. As can be seen in the diagram above, the first important step is the cultivation of self-awareness, which is the foundation of self-regulation, empathy, and compassion.

Being aware of awareness is something unique to humans. It is sometimes called meta-awareness. One tried-and-tested method to develop this capacity is through mindfulness; being aware of what is happening within, and around, us, while it is happening and to do so without resistance. We can develop this mindful awareness through many different types of meditation.

Learning to meditate can seem like a serious and possibly boring practice, bringing back all of our worst primary school memories: "Sit up straight, keep still, shut up, and concentrate!" This is the torment of most children, and as all of us still have an inner child cohabiting with our adult self, we often resist the perceived boredom of the practice. Learning compassion can also make it seem as if our practice is all about dealing with difficulties, which can seem very depressing!

Fortunately, this hasn't been my experience, and I hope it won't be yours.

On mindfulness retreats, I've often been astonished by the amount of laughter that arises when we look head-on at our self-destructive habits. Joy seems to bubble up out of nowhere once I recall that I am human, and not to blame for my struggles. Empathising with the difficulties of others forges friendships and creates connections that have carried me through life's changing seasons. And when I no longer need to hide my fear or vulnerability, then I can experience the freedom to let my emotions guide me in an authentic way of engaging with the people and the world around me.

When I have a good look at the things that my chattering, anxious, surface mind tells me, I could write a stand-up comedy show. It loves to catastrophise, to throw itself on the floor in a tantrum, to feel hard done by and self-righteous. And if I believe these thoughts, life is quite a rollercoaster. But when I hold that chaotic toddler-mind in awareness and observe those thoughts with a more expansive quality, then I can laugh at myself and develop a deep understanding of others as they go through the same moments. And they are moments; they do not linger, so long as I can see and release my grasp of them. The raw humour of human experience rises up to the surface, and I am free once again to connect with the sheer delight of inhabiting a human body.

This is what I have come to understand as holding space.

First, I learnt to hold space for my chaotic inner world, and to distinguish between thoughts that are harmful and those that provide momentary insights or guidance. And once I could trust that all thoughts, feelings, and physical sensations move through our awareness, like clouds through a vast sky, I had more capacity to hold space for others.

Instead of getting drawn into the grief, anger, or anxiety, of others, I've been learning how to stay present with their shifting emotional landscape and allow their insights to emerge within a felt sense of safety.

Another dimension of this happens in community. In peer-held spaces, we can change roles, from being held, to being the holder, depending on our moment-by-moment needs. In such spaces, I often feel the sense of resting back into community, or ancestry, or lineage, safe in the knowing that someone or something will be there as a back stop, whenever I feel depleted. This gives me the chance to resource myself before stepping back into whatever awaits.

Daily Meditation

Developing a daily meditation practice takes time and patience. It also requires sensitivity to your own past experiences.

For the many people who have experienced trauma, a silent sitting practice can be too triggering to begin with. You may need moving practices as a start, that release the tension from your body. This is where the Eastern healing practices like yoga or qi gong are so helpful, or the African and indigenous practices involving song, dance, and drumming. Before you can settle back into the sweet territory of silence, it may be necessary to sing, dance, and be held in community.

In this way, you allow your daily practice to develop according to your needs. The most important thing is to do something each day that allows you to cultivate self-awareness. Once we have the capacity to shift our trauma response to a peaceful response, we can bring all our passion to the work, without the fear of re-traumatising ourselves, or projecting our woundedness onto others.

> **Meditation App Suggestions**
>
> Insight Timer (a full range of traditions, including my own guided practices)
>
> Headspace (secular mindfulness, with a great starting programme for beginners)
>
> Liberate (by, and for, people of colour and indigenous practitioners)
>
> Centering Prayer (for Christian contemplation)
>
> MuslimPro (guidance for carrying out every day Islamic religious rituals)
>
> Calm or Breathe (calming and relaxation practices to down-regulate the nervous system)

Make sure your daily practice feels aligned with your own spiritual or religious beliefs and remember, it can take time to find what works for you. I've included some Meditation app suggestions above if you don't already have an established practice. Commit to building up over time from 5 minutes to 30 minutes of practice, in both the morning and evening. Starting with calming practices can help stabilise you, so you feel emotionally regulated before expanding your practice to gain insight into your habits and shadow side.

Rick Hanson, a neuropsychologist, has demonstrated through his research how we can use the mind to change the brain to change the mind for the better! All these simple mind-training practices, when done routinely, can activate a process known as experience-dependent neuroplasticity, which means that we can change the physical structure of our brain through daily practices of attention. Not only does this illustrate our own incredible ability to change our experience of ourselves, but we can also change the experiences of the world around us, by simply training our own mind with commitment and consistency.

There is so much to be aware of in each and every moment, but too often we're caught in habitual patterns of thinking. Or sometimes, we're focusing on one activity, and entirely unaware of other experiences. As humans, we tend to run on automatic pilot, which can be useful when navigating the complexities of daily life. However, opening to all the different fields of awareness, will help you tune in to the present moment in a much more meaningful way.

> ### Contemplative Practice: Fields of Awareness
>
> Find a comfortable way to sit, choosing to rest quietly and noticing all the fields of awareness that you can access. Be inquisitive, playful, and see what you discover as you go.
>
> The Senses – begin by becoming aware of your senses, in the present moment, learning to appreciate the full spectrum of life that comes in through the eyes, the ears, the nose, the mouth, and the sense of touch. Notice how the senses pick up information from the outside world, without attributing value to it. It is the mind that decides whether it is pleasant or unpleasant.
>
> Your Inner World – now shift to an interoceptive awareness, where you can get in touch with the subtle sensations of the muscles and bones, as well as your internal organs. Learn to stay aware of your body to gain an intuitive sense of the world around you. You have neuronal matter in the heart and gut, as well as the brain which means you are taking in information and energy from multiple sources all of the time.
>
> Your Emotional World – next get in touch with your emotions, moods, and feelings, without needing to change them. Bring awareness to the arising and dissolving of such experiences, without getting too involved or exhausted by them. An emotion is essentially a turbo-charged thought and can often be very strong, even in the body. By bringing kind awareness to your emotions, you start to realise that they pass when you don't interfere, allowing you to return to a natural state of calm, receptive awareness.
>
> The World of Thoughts – now get familiar with where your thoughts like to take you, be it into the past or the future, or commentating and analysing the present moment. Just as with emotions, you can stay interested in them, without getting involved. Over time, you may even be able to catch the moment when a thought arises and dissolves away, replaced by a new thought, and another, and another.
>
> Awareness of Awareness – this may feel like dropping in, or opening outwards. By experimenting, you allow yourself to see how it is to access

> a quality of awareness when you feel no need to do anything, because you can simply be with whatever arises and passes in your experience.
>
> Interconnectedness – finally, experiment with an awareness of the relational world, with people both near and far away. Many people have had profound experiences of their connections with others, such as when someone comes to mind, the phone rings, and it is them. This is a mysterious and magical field of awareness, and we will explore its potential more deeply as we continue our journey through this book.

Gratitude

The last 20 years have seen increasing interest in researching gratitude practices for their benefits to the individual, as well as for the social group.

Gratitude has been called the 'social glue' that supports relationships and underpins successful societies. It is defined as a two-step process whereby we recognise that we've received something of benefit, and that it has come from an external source. This external source can be another person, or a perceived higher power, or even nature. It is both a temporary emotion and an affective trait or disposition.

> *"More grateful people are happier, more satisfied with their lives, less materialistic, and less likely to suffer from burnout… Several studies have found that more grateful people experience less depression and are more resilient following traumatic events."*
> ~ Allen, 2018

All these aspects of gratitude can be supportive for changemakers, who are often exposed to traumatic incidents and have pro-social tendencies. Interestingly, gratitude has also been described as the 'mother of all virtues', and is supportive in cultivating the other virtues of patience, humility, and wisdom.

Something I find interesting about gratitude, is that it seems to navigate a skilful path between jealousy and guilt, both of which are emotions that originate from the comparing mind. Gratitude does this, in part, by recognising that there will always be people who are better off than we are, and there will always be people who are worse off. If we compare ourselves with others, we waste energy on emotions that serve no one. If we strengthen ourselves through gratitude, we have the inner resources we need to support those in difficult situations.

> ### Contemplative Practice: Gratitude
>
> Write down three things for which you are grateful today. You can write them on a Post-It or in a section of your journal. Keep this practice of making a daily list for the next next 10 weeks, and then read it out loud to yourself at the end.
>
> Becoming aware of small daily wonders and miracles, as well as the support we receive from others, can be an important step in finding the courage to face the uglier aspects of the world around, and within, us.

Engagement Practices

The next collection of practices we will explore together encourages participation in the world around us. In his work on Sacred Activism, Andrew Harvey lists several practices to prime the pump of engagement work. These are practices where we offer of ourselves to others, whether this involves giving of our presence, money, our talents, or time.

When we are faced with intransigent structural issues that cause harm in society, structural issues such as racism, sexism and xenophobia, they can feel too big causing us to back away, believing that there is nothing we can do to make a real and tangible difference.

However, the world is comprised of individuals, each operating within their own network. Good ideas tend to spread spontaneously and create a feeling of community cohesion. I recall watching just such a process take place online.

Someone I once met had her bike stolen in Brooklyn, New York. She desperately needed it to commute to her teaching job, so she put up a huge painted sign asking for the bike back. It produced a ripple effect through the community, and even got reported on in the national news. People came to her door offering consolation, bicycles, and donations.

Ultimately, she was not just able to replace her bike, she was also able to support a local women-run bike shop that helped to repair bicycles for community members. It was touching to witness how much happiness her big sign created; for those offering support and for the community who rallied together. There's something so comforting about witnessing the care of strangers, as it points to our essentially generous nature. It also serves as a reminder that many kind people are always close at hand, willing to help out at our time of need, as long as we are willing to ask.

Read through the suggested engagement practices below and see which one feels most accessible to you right now:

Support a Friend

Difficulties are part of every human life and it does not mean that we are doing something wrong. The support of a friend can be invaluable at such times, but it does need to be based on a deep understanding of their needs.

Years ago, I realised that a friend was struggling financially. Instead of asking what help she needed most, I transferred money into her account and let her know she could pay it back whenever her situation improved. This sort of assistance was not what she wanted, and it changed the relationship between us. It also put her further into debt, instead of helping her get out of it. My intention was kind, but it was not skilful. I learnt a lesson the hard way, losing a friend, instead of just taking time to listen to what would have helped her the most.

More recently, I called up a friend whose mother had just passed away, instead of sending a message or a voice note. I didn't need to say much, except, "How are you?", and she was able to relieve her pain just a little bit. She shared that many people seemed afraid to speak directly to her, because of the depth of her grief, and how comforting it was simply to know that she was being held in mind during this time. It was interesting for me to reflect that doing less seemed to be more helpful, perhaps because it was coming from a place of listening, rather than from wanting to fix an unfixable situation.

Once you feel strengthened by your contemplative practice, reach out to help others who might be grieving, ill, unemployed, or struggling with financial concerns. Notice how it feels to step into the role of caregiver and call your friend to ask whether you could ease their burdens in any way. Then reflect on how it felt to offer practical help and care, particularly if your offer of support is not well received.

Many of us do not feel comfortable to receive help, believing that to do so is a sign of weakness. So do not be surprised if your offer of help is rejected. If you are not attached to being thanked, then the potential for rejection will not matter. And if you are attached to the role of caregiving, then you might gain insight into your own habit pattern through the pain of rejection.

Change for Change

Keep small change in your pocket or, if you drive, keep coins or fruit in your car so you always have something to give to the people around you.

Andrew Harvey tells the story of giving change to a very old woman in India, who then used it to buy chapatis at a food stall. She divided the chapatis into two and shared it with a dog as emaciated as she was. Harvey was deeply touched by this cycle of giving from someone who had so little to share.

In South African cities, we have the opportunity to give to people at traffic lights every single day. Instead of feeling guilt, or pity, or judgement, towards the individuals, or anger at the situation that brought them onto the street, I've found it fulfilling to build relationships. I used to talk to two brothers standing at the traffic lights near my home. One day, when my bicycle chain fell off, the elder brother offered to assist me. During the pandemic, the brothers disappeared, and eventually only one came back. When I spoke to him, he shared the sadness of losing his brother, and his story really touched me.

At times, even when I have nothing to give, we still share a greeting and recognise the humanity within each other.

Donate a Meal

Choose to skip a meal one day this week and donate the money you save to an organisation of your choice, be it a soup kitchen or a community initiative that works to alleviate hunger or to support food sovereignty.

Even if the donated amount is small, don't forget the power of the collective. This practice is intended to shift your focus to the wellbeing of others. And, as we so often find, helping others can actually help us, as well.

> ### Engagement Practice: Choose and Do
>
> Choose one of the three engagement practices listed above. Start with what feels most manageable and see if you can carry it out with a genuine intention (not just because it is part of this course!). Then journal about how it felt to do it.
>
> Sometimes things do not go as we might hope. Our offers of help might miss the mark or even be rejected. This is useful material for reflection. Perhaps we did not have clear insight into the true needs of the other person, or we need to better understand our own underlying motivations.
>
> The reality for most of us is that we do not know how to offer help to others unconditionally.

Shadow Integration Work

My friend, Charlie Morley, is a wonderful lucid dreaming and Shadow Integration teacher, and he sums up shadow work in this way:

"The shadow was a term pioneered by the Swiss psychiatrist Carl Jung, to describe the parts of the unconscious mind that we have denied, disowned, or rejected. Jung called the shadow the 'dark side' of the human psyche: not dark as in bad, but dark as in not yet illuminated. The process of Shadow Integration involves shining the light of our conscious awareness into the shadows of our minds to tap into the energy that lies there. The shadow is a huge source of energy. The shadow is not bad. The shadow is simply the parts of ourselves that we are unwilling to love. The dark shadow is made up of our fear, our shame, our secrets, and our wounded heart. The golden shadow is made up of our talents, our blinding beauty, and our untapped potential (which we hide from others). To move into the shadow is to ask yourself, "What within me am I unwilling to love?" Shadow work is all about loving ourselves."

Charlie describes the process of Shadow Integration as getting to know our 'magnificent messiness'. Once we can see the shadow without judgement, we're able to integrate it making it possible to give others the opportunity to love themselves, and their own shadow, without judgement. In this way, we can integrate the wider shadow, known sometimes as the 'collective unconscious'.

So, why would we hide our golden shadow?

Identifying our unique talents, interests, knowledge, and passion, can be put to use as a source of inspiration for those around you, but it does require getting in touch with your authentic self. This then carries with it a responsibility. In South Africa, we often quote Marianne Williamson, as Nelson Mandela spoke her words in his inauguration speech in 1994:

> "Our deepest fear is not that we are inadequate.
> Our deepest fear is that we are powerful beyond measure.
> It is our light, not our darkness that most frightens us.
> We ask ourselves, 'Who am I to be brilliant, gorgeous, talented, fabulous?' Actually, who are you not to be?
> You are a child of God.
> Your playing small does not serve the world.
> There is nothing enlightened about shrinking so that other people won't feel insecure around you.
> We are all meant to shine, as children do.
> We were born to make manifest the glory of God that is within us.
> It's not just in some of us; it's in everyone.
> And as we let our own light shine, we unconsciously give other people permission to do the same.
> As we are liberated from our own fear, our presence automatically liberates others."
> ~ Marianne Williamson

It is our golden shadow that we can offer to others. We'll explore this more in Chapter 8 about 'A Life of Purpose'.

> **Shadow Integration Practice: Noticing Triggers**
>
> See if you can notice the times during your normal daily life when you feel triggered and what difficult emotions do you often experience? There may be two or three that repeat themselves, over and over again. Write them down, without any judgement. In a later section of the book, we'll gain a deeper understanding of why we have these difficult and destructive emotions. They are not your fault; they are an evolutionary necessity. They also point to where your needs are not being met.
>
> Nevertheless, you are responsible for investigating, understanding, integrating, and transforming them, and that can only happen when you turn to face them first.

HOME PRACTICES

1. This week, I invite you to focus on daily journaling. It is a form of meditation that can be a very powerful practice to develop self-awareness. This is of particular benefit to those with a speedy intellect, as it can be soothing to write out the mind's worries or ideas, get them on the page, and set them free. Journaling can be especially effective for changemakers who are exploring new systems or ways of engaging. By writing them down, they take on a life of their own, and finally come into being.

Journaling helps us listen to the surface chattering mind, and then drop below into our quiet wisdom self that is yearning to be heard. After a couple of pages of writing, I notice my own inner shift, and sometimes even a sense that the writing is happening through me.

It is a shift from the striving Doing mode of mind, to a more sensing Being mode, often associated with greater creativity and problem-solving. Author, Julia Cameron, describes this process as Morning Pages and she encourages her readers to write three pages every morning. For your own practice, you can choose the size of your journal depending on how much you like to write, but it must be three pages!

I, myself, have done this daily journaling practice often over the years, and inevitably find that it is only once I get to page three that the most valuable insights start to arise! We need to wade through quite a lot of residual thoughts and fanciful, distracting ideas, before our creativity can begin to see the light.

2. From the list given in the 'Foundational Practices' section, choose one calming practice that you'd like to do every day for a week and journal about your experience after each session.

You might like to use these journal-writing prompts:
- What physical sensations did you notice in your body?
- What emotions or moods did you witness?
- Were you able to identify any specific feelings and needs?
- Did your thoughts take you into the past or future, or did you find yourself analysing the present moment?
- How fast or slow did your thoughts move at the beginning compared to the end?
- Were you able to get the sense that your awareness is separate from the thoughts that move through it?

After a week, you could reflect on the longer-term impacts:
- How did it feel to take time for yourself during your busy life?
- How did the practice impact on your day?

CHAPTER 2

Circles of Safety

"The test of a civilisation is the way that it cares for its helpless members."
~ Pearl Buck

Self-Protection

The human nervous system has the remarkable capacity to keep us safe, through a process known as neuroception. Our Autonomic Nervous System (ANS) is continuously scanning the environment around us for cues of safety or danger. We absorb information subconsciously, through our senses, which then tells the body what action to take to stay safe.

The way we appraise our environment differs from person to person, depending on their life experiences. For example, on seeing a dog, one person may feel happy, and a wish to approach it, while another person might feel fear at the sight of the dog, and a wish to run away from the potential threat.

Additionally, these responses tend not to take the present moment into consideration. This particular dog might be friendly, or it might be vicious. It is our past associations that trigger the different reactions. By training in mindfulness, which hones our attention, we are able to see more clearly the reality of any situation and take appropriate action.

The process of neuroception involves the mind moving through a series of steps, most of which we are unaware:

1. We receive stimulus from the outer environment or our inner world e.g. a physical sensation, a sound, or a thought.
2. We appraise the stimulus as pleasant/safe, neutral, or unpleasant/unsafe.
3. We respond to the appraisal, and feel attracted to what seems pleasant or safe, taking limited to no notice of the neutral, and feeling aversion for the unpleasant or unsafe.
4. We react through actions or speech, moving towards what attracts us, ignoring the neutral, and moving away from, or resisting, what we are repelled by.

When you train your mind, you begin to see how much of your internal reactivity is based on past experiences. Slowly you'll learn to interrupt step four and even step three, but we will never be able to prevent the initial appraisal period of a stimulus because this is a survival necessity.

During a mindfulness practice, it is possible to watch the steps take place one after the other, and to feel the tendency to engage or react. And by doing so, we can start to become more and more skilful in choosing an appropriate response to our appraisal of a stimulus, rather than reacting based on conditioning. We learn to unlearn our unhelpful habits of mind and choose to live with a greater sense of freedom.

When I first moved to Johannesburg, a city that has a bad reputation for crime, I saw graffiti on a bridge that said, "Be Aware, not Afraid." This maxim has served me well when I walk the streets and through local parks. If my back tingles, like the hackles of a dog rising, I pay attention and do what I must to avoid danger. And if my heart stays open, I trust that felt sense and enjoy connecting with everyone I walk past.

> ## Contemplative Practice: Noting
>
> Today, let's work with the insight practice of open monitoring.
>
> After settling down by taking five deep breaths, open your field of awareness to your inner world and the outer world. Then ask yourself, "What is here? In my thoughts, my feelings, and my physical sensations, and in the world around me?"
>
> Silently note everything you become aware of – backache, birdsong, sadness, tingling, the sound of a passing car, tight breath, itch, cool breeze, anxiety, calm, 'To Do' list, etc.
>
> Then notice which sensations you find pleasant, neutral, or unpleasant, or which experiences make you feel safe or unsafe. You can even note, "Bird song - pleasant, police siren - unpleasant, breathing - neutral" to get familiar with how your mind appraises stimuli.
>
> Notice too if you try to cling onto the pleasant sensations, or push away the unpleasant ones, and how easy it is to lose touch with whatever you appraise as neutral. The breath, for example, is often ignored because we are so used to it, but once we bring attention to its regular, soothing flow, it may feel very sustaining and give us a sense of inner safety.

Responding to Danger

As mentioned, in Chapter 1, when we are threatened or harmed, and experience trauma, suffering, and disempowerment, we instinctively react in a few ways: fight, flight, freeze or flop. These hard-wired responses are expressed through a variety of different behaviours, such as armouring or blaming, suppression or denial, distraction or disconnection.

The fight and flight tendencies are action-oriented. They may not be skilful, thought-through actions, but we do at least have a sense of agency. With the freeze and flop responses, though, it can feel as though there's nothing we can do except cower, or stand rigid, like an animal hiding from its hunter.

Freezing is a normal, skilful response to extreme fear and trauma. In situations of life and death, it is vital, but it can have long-lasting consequences for the human mind, including dissociation, anxiety, and even Post-Traumatic Stress Disorder (PTSD). Immobility is the most difficult for us to work through as we lose the belief that we can interact with the world around us. This freeze response may also be held in place by negative self-beliefs, such as, "I can't do that, I am not good enough, I am not worthy."

The human brain is designed to coordinate action. We need to respond to disempowering situations; we're hard-wired for protective action. The freeze response traps us in many ways, both personally, and in our community or national roles:

- Depression – the 'black dog' that keeps us in bed or unable to move forward with our intentions.
- Disengagement, numbness, or overwhelm – when we give up before we've tried and cannot touch into the hope that arises through social action and connection.
- Bystander syndrome – where we hope, or assume, that someone else will act and choose to stand aside, even in the face of harm.
- Civil inaction – such as not voting or rejecting the structures set up to ensure democratic processes.

To shift from the disempowering way of relating to our life experience, it is useful to understand how to cultivate, and expand, our circles of safety.

Dimensions of Safety

I have identified six different dimensions of safety that seem relevant in my own life:
- Feeling safe with those who make us feel safe.
- Feeling safe within ourselves.
- Finding safety in a homogenous group.
- Finding safety in a diverse group, united by a shared vision.
- Feeling safe in threatening environments.
- Being a safe person for others when they feel unsafe.

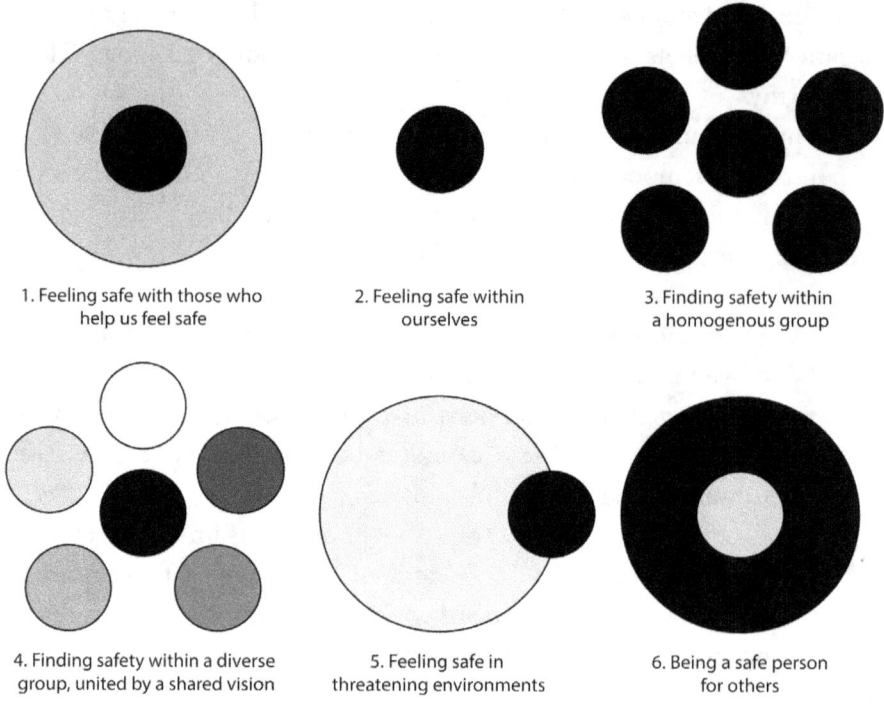

1. Feeling safe with those who help us feel safe
2. Feeling safe within ourselves
3. Finding safety within a homogenous group
4. Finding safety within a diverse group, united by a shared vision
5. Feeling safe in threatening environments
6. Being a safe person for others

Fig 4. Circles of Safety

Feeling safe with those who help us feel safe

We first learn what safety feels like when we are in the presence of someone who takes care of us. At best, they love us unconditionally and this allows for the development of our vitally important sense of secure attachment. When we feel loved and safe, the hormone oxytocin is released and we experience the felt sense of connection and contentment.

The loving caregiver may not always be a parent. Perhaps, for you, it was a nurse, or an aunt, or an adoptive parent, who was able to teach you how it felt to be loved and to feel safe. It is not important who played this role for you; what is important is to remember that someone did, otherwise you would not have survived.

Humans are born helpless, needing the care of another to survive beyond our early years. The reason that all of us are alive today is that many, many people have attended to our needs, and cared for us, particularly when we were young and at times of difficulty. We are embedded in community and part of an ecosystem of care.

Feeling safe within ourselves

The second dimension we need to develop is the feeling of internal safety. This can be cultivated consciously through mindfulness and self-compassion practices, through which we learn to befriend ourselves, and speak to ourselves in a kind and understanding way. We also learn to counteract experiences of threat, or constant drive, with a soothing, supportive voice tone, and a caring inner dialogue.

Many people feel self-hatred and regularly criticise themselves. They talk to themselves in a way that they would never talk to another for fear of losing the friendship. We need to learn to become our own supportive friend. Even negative mental habits, such as self-criticism and self-loathing, can be alleviated over time by recognising that we are all flawed and make mistakes. It is a common attribute of being human!

To sustain ourselves, we need to shift regularly from our sympathetic nervous system response of fight and flight to our parasympathetic nervous system response of rest, digest, tend, and befriend. Learning simple practices that down-regulate our nervous system gives us the chance to feel internal safety and friendliness.

These practices include deep soothing breaths, mindful movement practices, and singing or chanting. All of these increase our vagal tone, which carries messages of safety along one of our cranial nerves, known as the vagus nerve.

Contemplative Practice: Self-Soothing

Sit quietly, with a strong back and a soft, open front. Either let your breath deepen a little or feel the points of contact with the surface beneath you. Now bring your hand to your heart area, stroking your chest, or giving yourself a hug. Feel how the body responds to the sense of caring touch. As much as possible, speak to yourself in a kind and soothing way, saying, "It's ok, whatever I'm feeling, it's ok. Let me take care of myself in this moment."

Finding safety within a homogenous group

As social animals, humans experience a sense of belonging in groups, particularly those groups in which we feel that people are like us. From an evolutionary perspective, we tend to trust, and be attracted to, people who look or sound like us, and feel cautious around those who are different. This has survival benefits but has also been a frightening source of in-group/out-group conflict, racism, and xenophobia.

We are hard-wired to focus attention on our in-group and feel a sense of allegiance in order to feel safe. It's important to remember though, that we have three co-existing dimensions of our identity: the 'I', the 'we' and the 'all of us'. One is not better than the others; they're all necessary aspects of our personal and collective identity. We can value the importance of a group identity, while still moving beyond it and touching into the identity of being human, rather than being one type of human.

These in-groups may be family or religious groups, support, or affinity groups. Support groups, like Alcoholics Anonymous, are of great importance when people have been through addiction and other difficult life experiences. Affinity groups give us an opportunity of connecting with others on the basis of shared identities, such as race or sexual orientation. Some people come into activism as a response to a trauma or a situation that has impacted them personally. This is often where a support group or affinity group can be a very powerful aid for them to heal amongst people who identify with the same structural issues or circumstances that caused them harm in the first place.

However, we need to be careful not to use affinity groups as a way of reinforcing stereotypes or perpetuating in-group/out-group bias. It is too easy to fall into habits of othering, where we feel a sense of 'us and them'. Affinity or support groups are best run as a place to feel belonging and unconditional support. They give us the confidence to move out beyond our sphere of safety and tap into the understanding of our common humanity. Group meetings offer a place of safety, yet ultimately, we can leave them behind. We need to form bridges to other groups and prevent the tendency to perpetuate the binary of 'us' and 'them'.

If you are working through this book as part of a group, it will be an important sanctuary for a time, but you can leave the group behind when the course comes to an end or whenever you want to move in a new direction.

Finding safety in a diverse group, guided by shared principles

You may be part of a group that is diverse in terms of age, race, or religious beliefs, and you might have been drawn together by shared principles, such as a community group, an NGO, or a residents' association. These can be challenging places to practice deep listening to viewpoints that may differ from your own, while still acknowledging the shared principles that encouraged the group to form. Reminding the group of these principles can help maintain a sense of safety, even at times of strong debate and disagreement.

NGOs, schools, or spiritual communities can be complex places as their members have co-existing motivations, which are not always fully acknowledged. There is the overriding wish to do good, and to be altruistic, yet we are still flawed human beings and must meet our basic needs as well. Sometimes that means competing for what we perceive as scarce resources with other organisations, or spending hours on fund-raising, when we want to be in the field, seeing the fruits of our work.

The human tendencies of jealousy, frustration, and greed sideswipe us, and there is often sharp emotional conflict. NGOs are not always the loving, caring places they may wish to be. It is the same in schools, supposedly places with a shared vision of helping children to flourish yet wrought with internal politics and reactivity. Churches and spiritual centres, too, can be filled with conflict and human unskillfulness.

People are people and we trigger each other when we do not fully understand our own needs, and we're guided by our unseen shadow aspects. Therefore, we need to keep remembering our values, while working on integrating our shadow material.

Feeling safe in threatening environments

The fifth dimension of safety involves knowing that we can feel safe enough in ourselves to go out into the world, often into conditions that could be potentially harmful or threatening. This is the life of the spiritual warrior who is able to stay open to the outside world, even when they are threatened.

Many climate justice activists are under threat from multinational corporations, yet they continue to act, believing that the cause is worth the consequence. The spiritual warrior has a strong internal sense of safety, honed through years of practice. When we lose our ego-centric focus through meditation, nothing can harm us, as there is no sense of self to be harmed.

This is the journey that some compassionate activists take as great courage can arise in the presence of compassion.

Being a safe person for others

Once you have cultivated these dimensions of safety within yourself, you can provide a place of safety for others. Holding space for others is a valuable gift that allows the healing we need to engage skilfully with the world.

Perhaps you feel supported by a higher power, or a sense that within everyone there is innate goodness that will reveal itself under the right conditions. To provide safety for others, you'll need to ensure you are also holding space for, and continually resourcing, yourself.

> **Engagement Practice: Dimensions of Safety**
>
> Copy the diagram (Fig 4) into your notebook. Label yourself in each diagram, and label those:
> - With whom you feel safe,
> - Who are part of your homogenous group,
> - Who are part of a diverse group you belong to,
> - Who seem to pose a threat to you, and
> - You provide safety to.
>
> Now ask yourself: "How do I provide a sense of safety for myself?"

Disturbing Emotions

There are many ways of categorising emotion. Western psychology focuses on seven universal human emotions: anger, fear, sadness, disgust, contempt, surprise, and happiness. What tends to make us feel unsafe are the disturbing or destructive emotions we all have to work with. These are also explored extensively in Buddhist psychology and they're destructive in that they can damage relationships if not attended to with skill and presence of mind.

All the emotions we describe as negative have an evolutionary purpose. Anger and fear relate to fight and flight. Anger helps us remove obstacles, while fear motivates us to escape from threat. Sadness draws out caring from others, to create connections in the face of loss. Disgust provides motivation to get rid of something that could be poisonous or harmful to us or to our group, while contempt is a way to assert superiority within a group's hierarchy.

On the positive end of the emotion scale, happiness deepens our connections and willingness to cooperate, while surprise helps to focus our attention on something unexpected or unknown. This enables us to create new neural pathways in the brain and explains why curiosity and wonder are considered such beneficial qualities in mind training. These particular emotions arise in response to our instinctual tendency to appraise our environment, and to protect the survival of our species.

Buddhist psychology uses the term klesha to describe destructive emotions, or 'mind poisons'. Yet there is no sense of getting rid of these emotions, rather transforming them into useful qualities. The five main mind states that cause us harm, and potentially harm others, are hatred, arrogance, greed, jealousy, and ignorance. We all have them, although we might try to hide them because of our social conditioning; we've been taught they harm relationships, so we try to push them down, rather than learning how to recognise, name and admit to these emotions, without acting on them.

Meeting My Mind Poisons

My first 10-day meditation retreat came about when I was working in Thailand after the tsunami. My father had recently died, and I was finding it hard to recognise myself. My productivity had declined drastically, and I felt a strong urge to run away from all responsibility. When an email about a 10-day retreat came through, that was to be held in silence, I felt it was the time out that I needed. I signed up immediately, took leave, and set off a week later.

The physical journey took four hours, by bus and long-tailed boat, to a floating retreat venue on the Rajjaprabaa Dam in Surathani Province. It was an idyllic venue for the start of my inner journey.

Under normal circumstances, I would have resisted the idea of silence. I would've wanted to try and get to know everyone on the first evening. However, I was emotionally drained and was looking forward to companionship without the effort of conversation.

During the first few days, my lips were sealed, and I would smile, but look down if others greeted me. Several of the participants were less quiet, the retreat being but one part of their holiday adventure in Thailand, and I soon noticed an inner disapproving 'tut tut' each time I heard laughter or a whispered conversation. A feeling of arrogance began to creep up behind me, as I felt more and more proud of my diligent adherence to the retreat rules.

One morning we were in a sitting practice when a family of otters started playing on a log that was floating past the meditation platform. Some of us turned quietly to witness this performance of joy and freedom. Then, in a flash, the 'noisy girl' who had been caught up in her own thoughts and not heard the splashes, whipped her head round and shouted out, frightening away the otter family. I no longer felt pride of being the good student, but fury at her inconsiderate stupidity. She had spoiled my fun by scaring away my otters. I felt the heat of anger swelling in my chest and had to actively attempt to stifle it as the urge to let it burst out of my mouth arose. Fortunately, we were brought back to the breath and the loving kindness metta practice by the retreat facilitators. The anger subsided in its own time, and my perspective shifted. I came to realise that I could have – and likely would have – been that distracted, noisy girl at any earlier stage in my life.

The following morning, I woke up and made my way towards the showers, located on an island, across a wobbly, rustic bridge. I waited, while someone came in the other direction and cast my eyes down to prevent a spoken greeting. As I took my turn to cross the bridge, my foot slipped on the wet planks, and the first word to come through my lips was 'F * * K'.

I was mortified, and spontaneously imagined a hand of God – a big blow-up pointy-fingered hand – coming out of the sky to draw attention to my judgemental thoughts and mindlessness. It felt like instant karma that had almost seen me dunked into the lake.

A huge inner laugh erupted within me at the absurdity that the normally chatty student was now the one who was the 'silence' monitor. I realised how freely I attributed instant punishment to a wrathful god, yet never believed in the kind counterpart, who would answer prayers. And so, with one trip, and a near swim, I was able to realise my own need to take responsibility for the thoughts coursing through my mind, rather than blaming bad things on a source outside of myself.

These two mind poisons - anger and pride - are still regular visitors, who try to dunk me into the lake whenever I'm being judgemental or self-righteous. And I try to welcome them these days, with a little less horror and a little more humour. Having acknowledged that they are part of every human life, I see that I am neither particularly good, nor particularly bad.

I'm just a normal person being human.

> ### Shadow Integration Practice: Identifying Your Disturbing Emotions
>
> See if you can identify your two most commonly arising disturbing emotions.
>
> How do they help you to see when you are out of alignment or judging others? You can also view them in terms of their evolutionary necessity. When you feel anger, for example, is it because it is hiding fear and a sense of being threatened?
>
> Keep a watchful eye on these disturbing emotions throughout the day and write about them in your journal. What sorts of situations give rise to them? And how do you respond to them when you notice their arrival?

Transforming Disturbing Emotions

By practising emotion regulation, our disturbing emotions can be taken care of. This is when the top brain, the prefrontal cortex, can witness what is happening in the limbic system, without being ruled by it.

One of my yoga teachers talks about the limbic system as a fractious child. We want to put the child in the back seat, safely held in place by a seatbelt. It wouldn't be right to put him or her in the boot, or indeed, to let the child drive. Our emotions can often feel like the child-like part of ourselves, craving attention, but they need to be responded to with kindness and a sense of holding.

Alan Wallace and Shauna Shapiro have explored four steps to help people find emotional balance. It becomes possible to transform our negative emotions through conative, attentional, cognitive, and emotional balance, as well as increasing constructive emotional engagement.

Conative balance relates to the motivation to achieve balance. This requires a commitment, so we don't give in to apathy. It includes intentions, aspirations, and vows, which provide propulsion for the next three types of balance.

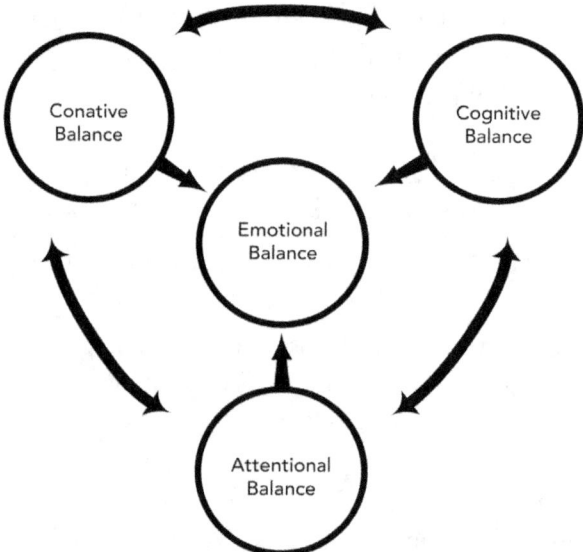

Fig 5. A Model for Emotional Balance

Attentional balance can be cultivated in the ways we've been learning, through simple breath and meditation practices, that develop relaxation, stability, and vivid attention.

Cognitive balance implies relating to the world moment-by-moment, without conceptual assumptions and expectations. This requires developing a curiosity for, and insight into, our habitual tendencies, through insight or reflection practices. These three balances support us in terms of achieving emotional balance, where we can use the emotions that we feel for gathering information, without being ruled by them.

Buddhist psychology recognises that once we bring a sense of friendliness to our disturbing emotions, holding them in mindful awareness, they dissolve away. We learn to regulate emotions from the top down, which eventually means that they disappear from the bottom up.

When you first start to practice, you will experience difficult emotions repeatedly, and slowly develop the confidence of feeling them, without reacting to them. Over time, you may even find yourself in situations where you once might have reacted with anger or jealousy, and yet you now feel calm and balanced. This is when we know that the transformation has started to take place, from the bottom up.

With practice, even the most destructive emotions can transform into wisdom, and this is a wonderful motivation to keep bringing friendliness and compassion to our unskillfulness, again and again. The transformational process is summed up in the table below. Hatred, or anger, is said to be the most commonly arising disturbing emotion. It causes pain to the one feeling it, and if not attended to, can cause harm to others through aggression. If, however, we can purify our hatred, then it transforms into mirror-like wisdom, which allows us to see things accurately, without distortion, and to make decisions accordingly. This allows anger to become a powerful impetus to personal or social transformation, without the damage caused by hatred or rage.

Pride or arrogance occur when we feel that we are better than others. We judge the things we do as good, and what others do as bad, and we cannot learn from others when we feel superior. When we can purify and transform our arrogance, we do not judge things, or separate ourselves from others, but rather experience everything through the wisdom of equality.

Disturbing Emotion	Wisdom Quality
Anger or Hatred	Mirror-like Wisdom
Pride or Arrogance	Wisdom of Equality
Attachment, Greed or Desire	Discerning Wisdom
Jealousy or Envy	All-accomplishing Wisdom
Ignorance	Wisdom of the Highest State

Desire or greed can cause us to suffer by keeping our minds restless and unsatisfied. When desire is transformed into its wisdom energy, we're able to understand all living beings and appreciate their qualities. This is discerning wisdom, which arises in the presence of contentment.

Jealousy includes the dimensions of envying the wealth, good fortune, and success of others. When we are trapped by jealousy, we cannot find our own sense of well-being, because we keep looking at those who have more. We find that our minds are always comparing us with others. With the purification of this disturbing emotion, jealousy spontaneously transforms into all-accomplishing wisdom, because all of our wishes can be achieved effortlessly when we tap into the skills and the support of others.

The negative emotion of ignorance is the hardest to transform because we do not know what we do not know. This requires sustained and consistent practice to get to know our own mind, and all of the games that it plays. Transforming ignorance gives us access to the highest states of wisdom, which sees all things as they truly are. Therefore, we can use engagement work as a way to identify where we still need to transform our shadow aspects or our mind poisons.

If we stay alone in a meditation cave, how will we ever know that we still have work to do on the inside?

Transforming Painful Emotions

RAIN is a powerful contemplative practice that you can use to cultivate a sense of inner safety, particularly at a time of difficulty or when a painful emotion arises. It takes its name from the acronym:

R – Recognising
A – Allowing
I – Intimately Attending
N – Nurturing

When we experience difficulty, our instinct is to turn away and hope it goes. This practice asks for a counterintuitive response; to turn towards whatever we are feeling, and to recognise, label, or name our experience. By doing this, we allow it to be present. After all, it is here already, even if we don't like it. This does not mean condoning it or over-indulging in the feeling, rather allowing the experience to be here, without pushing it away. Allowing does not even require acceptance, it simply means that we're holding a space for the presenting emotion to exist.

Next, we bring our intimate attention to how the experience is felt in the body, heart, and mind, and for each physical sensation, feeling or thought, we again recognise and allow. Anger may be the presenting emotion, but maybe there is also hurt, or despair or hopelessness beneath it. It is like a lid on a pot. When we take off that lid and look below, can we see complete heartbreak? Is that, perhaps, what we are connecting with?

Finally, we realise that we can be both the one suffering, and the one who is taking care. We nurture ourselves and offer self-compassion, particularly when discovering the wounded child within us, as we give ourselves the love we needed at a stage in life when we were wounded.

It can be helpful to listen to the RAIN recording on my website, so you can experience the practice fully. Alternatively, you may ask a friend to read it to you. This can also support you in feeling a little safer as you get to know the practice.

Contemplative Practice: RAIN

Begin by sitting or lying comfortably. Feeling a connection to the ground and remembering that it is a reliable place to come back to, whenever emotions trigger us. Get the sense of being held by the earth beneath you.

Now centre your attention on the breath, as it flows in and out. Taking five deep breaths and allow them to release slowly and gently. This is an anchor to return to if your mind is carried off. Being mindful does not mean being in the present all the time, but just returning to the present again and again.

Now allow your mind to select a difficulty from the last week or month, and recreate it in your mind's eye, picturing the faces or the words that were said. You may even begin to feel, in this moment, the emotions that came up at the time.

The first step is to recognise the presenting emotion. What were you experiencing in that moment? Can you give it a name? Allow it to be here. You've invited it back into this moment, and you have recreated what you felt during the original incident.

Bring an intimate attention to the experience. How do you feel? What is happening in your body? Any tightening or shortness of breath? Do your shoulders cave in or is there a knot in your stomach? How does the body respond to difficulty? Allow it to be felt as physical sensation.

Now bring your intimate attention to the heart, noting what feelings are underneath, or around, the presenting emotion. Sometimes they're the feelings you may not be so comfortable to name, such as shame, or abandonment, or not being seen, or understood. Recognise and allow all the feelings and emotions rising in this moment.

Next move your attention to the world of thoughts. What was going on in your mind at the time? What sort of stories were you telling yourself? Do you notice yourself solidifying, saying 'I always..." or "I never..."? Remember that thoughts arise spontaneously. You cannot control them. There's no need to criticise yourself or feel ashamed of thoughts that emerge. You simply need to recognise them and allow them to be here.

You may have got in touch with a tender and vulnerable part of yourself, like an inner child. Now offer yourself a sense of nurturing. As you take care, realise that you are constantly in a flow of change – learning new skills, doing things differently. Nothing is solid. What may have seemed like a mistake or difficulty may bring a new insight, or even a sense of clarity around your values. Nurturing is a powerful aspect of self-care. Listen to your own tone of voice. How do you talk to yourself at a time of difficulty? See if you can invite a soothing and gentle voice tone.

When you feel ready, very gently, notice yourself once again connected to the earth. Feel the breath flowing in and out. In your own time, allow your eyes to reopen. The intention of this practice is not to find a solution to your difficulty. Rather, it is to provide a holding space for it, as it moves through you, in its own time.

Forgiveness

Revenge is described as a fundamental human emotion and the tendency to retaliate or seek retribution seems to be hard-wired into us as a survival mechanism. However, revenge is rarely equitable, and it can set off a vicious cycle of vengeance, which in some cases, continues for generations. Returning harm for harm's sake is a basic human approach to justice, but it correlates with the lower end of Lawrence Kohlberg's moral development scale. As humans committed to evolving our consciousness, we can do much better than that.

Forgiveness research has revealed that people who forgive others more readily report less anxiety, depression, and hostility; they're less likely to ruminate and more likely to be empathic. Just like generosity, it is the one who forgives (or gives) that seems to experience the most benefit from the act, both in terms of developing pro-social personality traits and living a more fulfilling life.

Contemplative Practice: Forgiveness

Recall someone who has recently betrayed you or hurt you. Without trying to rush the process, commit to the first step of opening up a little, with the longer-term wish of forgiving them. This process is not for their benefit and does not mean that justice is forgotten; rather it is to free ourselves from holding onto resentment and anger, both of which restrict our heart's ability to open anew.

As you experiment with opening, little by little, insights may arise such as the idea that they probably only caused you harm because they were also suffering. This does not excuse their behaviour; it allows you to understand our common human difficulties. We all have caused harm to others when we were feeling cornered or out of alignment with our true selves.

You might like to wish for this person to discover their own life purpose, and their capacity for goodness and joy. This helps connect us with our own capacity for compassion.

HOME PRACTICE

1. During your journaling, you may have found that you focus on the difficulties of your life, rather than on the things that are going well. This is normal. We all have what is called a 'negativity bias', which is part of our survival instinct. The brain learns very quickly from difficult experiences because it wants to be able to protect us in the future.

To balance out this tendency, we need to keep a watchful eye on all the things that are going well, or for which we are grateful. Keep going with your gratitude practice from the first chapter and see if you can identify what your values are. When does gratitude most often arise for you? Keep a record throughout the week and see what patterns you notice.

2. You can do the RAIN practice as part of a formal sitting meditation, or you can also experiment with it in the heat of the moment. If you find yourself triggered this week, see how it feels to go swiftly through the steps, recognizing your emotion and letting it stay. Notice what happens in your body, heart and head while the emotion is present, and see whether you can bring a sense of nurturing understanding to yourself before you react to the situation.

CHAPTER 3

Ways to Engage

*"Let your vision be as vast as space,
and your actions as fine as flour."*
~ Padmasambhava

In this chapter, we will journey through the different dimensions of an engaged life, so that you can choose how best to contribute to the world around you. The dimensions are like fractals; the properties do not change despite the scale. All dimensions of engagement are carried out with the wish to help beings, whether we focus on it at the level of family, community, or the world. Our intention stays steady, whatever the level of magnification.

You can engage:
- As an individual, noticing how a well-timed comment or a random act of kindness can make a big difference in someone's day.
- Within a family, offering children a safe and supportive upbringing that prevents many of the problems that get projected onto others later on in life.

- In the workplace, by creating safe, joyful, and sustainable businesses, where the need to make a profit is balanced against other motivating factors.
- In community, making direct changes and influencing policy through your local structures. At this level, you may well rub shoulders with people from outside your familiar circle of safety and this can help you expand your capacity for understanding.
- Nationally and globally, where it is often difficult to notice that genuine change is taking place, so we need to maintain hope and trust that structural changes happen, as individuals within the structure change.

"Do your little bit of good where you are;
it's those bits of good put together that overwhelm the world."
~ Archbishop Desmond Tutu

During the different stages of your life, you may find yourself playing different roles. Young people tend to be on the frontline of societal and structural change, as they have great passion, a willingness to take risks or disrupt the status quo, and fewer responsibilities to others. As you move through stages of having a family or a community that depends on you, you may need to step back and provide support in a less confrontational way. As an older, or retired person, you can be a wisdom keeper, offering what you have learnt in life to others so that they can learn from your experience, rather than from making mistakes. The world is changing so swiftly, however, that a wisdom keeper's main role is probably that of deep listener.

In 2021, I attended a protest in Oxford, in the United Kingdom, with a dear friend who is a committed and compassionate activist. The protest was organised by university students, so we decided to adopt the role of the older activist aunties! We made extra cardboard placards and offered them to anyone who wished to join. When the photo appeared in the BBC news, our placards were in evidence, and we were just out of the shot. It felt right to be the invisible support for the next generation, while contributing our time and energy in a supportive and tangible way.

The breadth of our impact is not as important as our wholehearted intention. Our interconnectedness means that every action carried out with the wish to benefit others can have a far-reaching influence.

You may be a parent, wanting to raise children who have the awareness, adaptability, and creativity, to cope with their future world. Perhaps you are the leader of a company or a non-profit organisation. The scale at which you work depends on your personality and your skillset. Your impact can be enormous if you keep focused on moment-by-moment actions, guided by altruistic intention.

Greta Thunberg, the young Swedish climate justice activist is a living example of this truth. By sitting outside the Parliament every Friday on a school strike, she has mobilised millions of people, both young and old, across the globe.

> **Contemplative Practice: Interconnectedness**
>
> Find a comfortable way to sit, feeling your body resting down onto the surface beneath. Bring to mind your intention of connecting, across space and time, with all those who are impacted in some way by your life, and those whose lives have impacted yours. This is the truth of interconnectedness.
>
> Allow your breath to flow effortlessly in and out, until you begin to feel a little more settled. Feel into your spine, noticing perhaps how it elongates a little as you breath in, and softens down as you breath out. Each vertebra moves slightly as part of the whole, each vertebra is needed as part of the whole spine.
>
> Now imagine your friends and family members, and their friends and family members, reaching out in ever widening circles across the world. You are part of a web of interconnectedness with other humans, animals, insects, and the earth itself.
>
> Now let an image of your father come to mind, whether you knew him or not. Imagine your father and his family standing behind your right shoulder. Picture your mother and your mother's family standing behind your left shoulder. Sense into that connection across time.
>
> In your imagination, follow your ancestral lineage back to the beginning of human life on earth, like two enormous wings behind you, with the tips touching. Sense that the first breath of the first people has been

> passed all the way from ancient time, through to this present moment, and the breath you are taking right now. You are connected to all who have gone before, and all who will come after you, whether by blood, marriage, or intention.
>
> As you bring the practice to a close, soften into the feeling of interconnectedness, across time and space. You are never alone; your ancestors live within you. Now rest for a while in simple mindfulness of the present moment, perhaps basking in the warmth of interconnectedness.

Gentle Protest

Engaging with the many issues in the world around you does not mean you need to call yourself an 'activist'. The stereotype of the extroverted, marching activist, often excludes the people who similarly care deeply about social and climate issues. Now, more than ever, the world needs an expansive and inclusive approach where engagement is accessible to everyone.

Sarah Corbett, in the United Kingdom, and Stacey Rozen in South Africa, are both craftivists. In their respective TED talks, they explore ways of including gentle, quiet activists in social change movements. Repetitive handiwork, such as embroidery or crochet, is therapeutic and allows participants the chance to contemplate issues of social and climate justice in a place of safety. Stacey also explores the word 'yarn' – the thread and the story – both of which are vital in the roles that craftivists play.

Introverts are often deep thinkers, who are willing to share ideas with others in a non-threatening environment. It is intimate activism, based on listening to the people they disagree with, or being a critical friend, rather than an oppositional enemy. While it can be slow, one-on-one sharing of information, the stories often move swiftly through social media.

Stacey's #10millionmasks initiative spread through Southern Africa and into Australia and New Zealand in a very short time, while Sarah's Canary Craftivist project mobilised diverse communities, leading up to COP26 in Glasgow.

While introverts may wish to avoid conflict, they can be of strategic importance when negotiating with power holders. Provocative street art, or handkerchiefs embroidered with messages, help to intrigue people, and create opportunities for dialogue and conversations.

If we approach everyone in an aggressive way, we can trigger their threat response and set up cycles of conflict, resulting in an unwillingness to engage in dialogue. Craftivism is an example of delicate, relational activism, through which we can tap into what inspires people, while sensing into their values and seeing their potential for good.

Tithing

The practice of tithing is part of most spiritual traditions. In Judaism, it is known as maaser, in Islam as zakat, and in Buddhism, it is the practice of dana or generosity. The word 'tithe' means a tenth so this is an invitation to donate 10% of your income to a cause of your choice. It can also be a chance to donate 10% of your time or skills in service of those around you. You can either choose one cause and investigate how supporting this over time moves you, or you can choose different causes each month to reflect your different areas of concern. Tithing is an ancient tradition, which seems to work at multiple levels. We can explore three different benefits:

- We get to practice generosity as an antidote for greed and attachment.
- We get to make someone else feel happy by giving to them, or giving to an organisation, so that it can perform the work that will support others. Their happiness is contagious.
- We benefit from planting positive seeds. At our times of financial worry, we can feel protected by the tithe. The giving away of anything sets in motion its return.

The first benefit sees the tithe as an opportunity to counteract the disturbing emotion of greed through generosity. I've always felt comfortable giving away my time, but have felt that limiting voice, "Not enough", echoing through my mind when it comes to giving away money. Rational arguments always pop up about saving for later life. Yet, when I've honoured the tithe, I've also experienced those unexpected moments in which a source of income appears, just at the time I needed it most.

Seeing someone else happy can be a powerful source of joy for us as well. Knowing that we've been part of a programme that supports others can give a sense of meaning and purpose to our lives. Research by Cortland

Dahl and Richie Davison reveals that a sense of purpose is one of the most robust predictors of psychological well-being.

My friend and colleague, Felicity Joan Hart, describes the tithe as supportive protection. It can be seen as a way of tapping into the positive aspects of karma. The term karma is often interpreted as negative i.e. if you harm someone, you will in turn be harmed. However, in Buddhism, it is viewed as a clear, mathematical formula. If you plant wholesome seeds, nourishing plants grow; if you plant noxious weeds, poisonous plants will grow. Say something unkind and it will bounce back. Be kind and your kindness will return at the time you need it. There is no judge involved, no retribution, just a sense that the energy or intention we put out to the world, boomerangs back at some point in the future.

This is like practising gratitude. It seems to begin a whole cycle of experiencing more of what we are grateful for. There are many ways to explain this, but the least mystical is that we train our attention.

If we are focusing our minds on acts of kindness, for example, we start noticing more and more. We can recognise when people are kind to us, and appreciate it, rather than brushing it off. This makes sense in the same way that when we are thinking of buying a specific make of car or phone – we tend to start seeing them everywhere! They were always there, it's just that our attention is now tuned in to seeing things more clearly.

So, the tithe, in turn lays the foundation for that return flow, the feeling that there is always enough to give; we will enjoy the act of giving and we can also learn to stay open to times when we need to receive. You might also start being aware of the mysterious power of giving; it seems to set a flow in motion, and as we give, we receive more, to give more.

Try it out for yourself!

Be careful, though, if you are someone who tends to give everything away to the point that you end up feeling depleted or unable to support yourself, you may need to tithe to yourself. In a 24-hour day, I try to tithe 2.4 hours to my spiritual practice, whether that is through meditation, movement, or journaling.

You may even need to tithe 10% of your income to yourself, so that you don't feel a sense of lack. The skill comes in noticing what your habitual tendencies are, and counteracting them in a systematic way, until you find that you are back in balance.

> ### Engagement Practice: Tithing
> Try tithing this week. Calculate how much you have earned and offer 10% to a cause that is close to your heart. If you have not earned an income, then offer 10% of your time.
>
> Write about how you feel as you go through the process.

Different Roles of the Activist

A healthy forest is a diverse forest. A thriving forest needs trees of different species and ages to sustain the lives of all the insects and animals that are also needed in the ecosystem. In the natural world, diversity is strength. In the social world, this is also true, even if it means that we need to learn more skills of inclusion, deep listening, and understanding varied viewpoints.

Deepa Iyer, a racial justice activist, writer, and lawyer in the United States, has produced some powerful work on social change ecosystems. She writes about how all of us, in our daily lives, or as part of movements and organisations, play different roles in the pursuit of equity, liberation, inclusion, and justice.

We can, and must, be an activist forest, thriving through our diversity. She explains the different roles of the activist as follows:

- Weavers who see the through-lines of connectivity between people, places, organisations, ideas, and movements.
- Experimenters who innovate, pioneer, and invent; who take risks and course correct as needed.
- Frontline Responders who address community crises by marshalling and organising resources, networks, and messages.
- Visionaries who imagine and generate our boldest possibilities, hopes and dreams, and remind us of our direction.
- Builders who develop, organise, and implement ideas, practices, people, and resources in service of a collective vision.
- Caregivers who nurture and nourish the people around by creating and sustaining a community of care, joy, and connection.
- Disruptors who take uncomfortable and risky actions to shake up the status quo, to raise awareness, and to build power.

- Healers who recognise and tend to the generational, and current, traumas caused by oppressive systems, institutions, policies, and practices.
- Storytellers who craft and share our community stories, cultures, experiences, histories, and possibilities, through art, music, media, and movement.
- Guides who teach, counsel, and advise, using their gifts of well-earned discernment and wisdom.

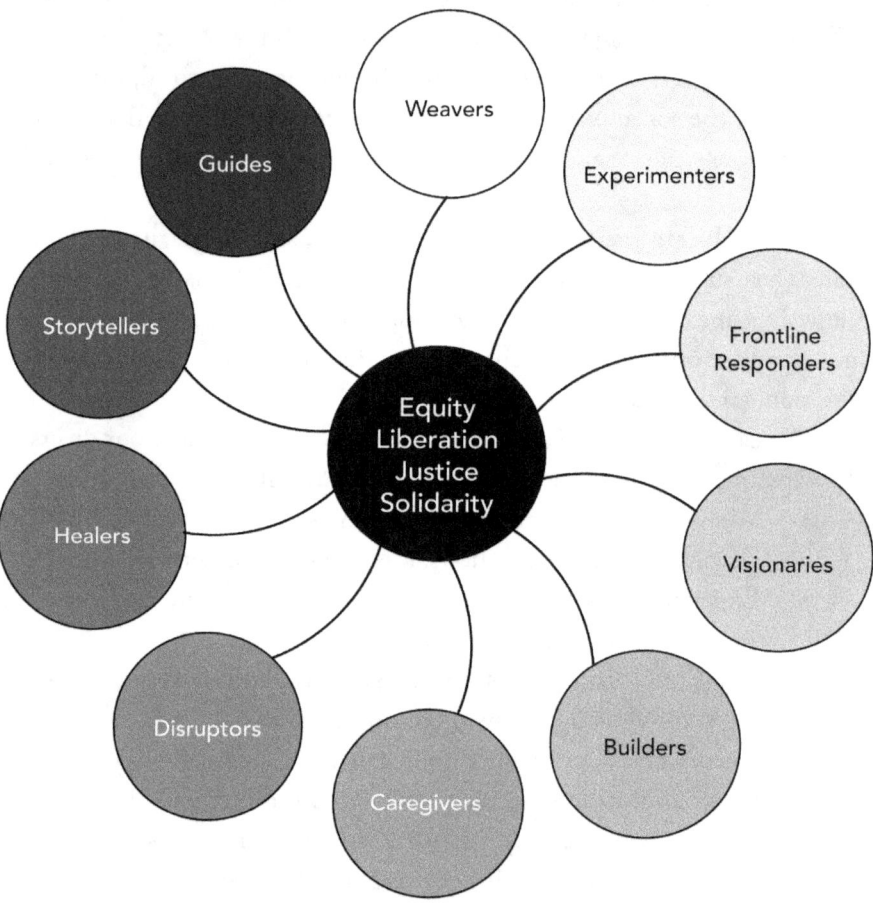

Fig 6. The Social Change Ecosystem Map
Attribution: @2018 Deepa Iyer, Building Movement Project

Deepa reassures us that not everyone can (or should) play all of these roles. At times, we may even find ourselves switching between different roles, depending on personal and external circumstances. Parents of young children may need to move back from the frontlines for a while in order to bring up a future-fit family. We might be observers and supporters on the side from time-to-time, particularly if we need to take care of our health or energy. An effective, healthy, and sustainable social change ecosystem requires different actors to play each of these different roles, and often, at different times.

We need to be patient and adopt a multi-pronged approach, using legal means, or political or social, whichever best serves the issue at that time. We also need to allow ourselves to play just one role, without worrying that it isn't enough.

When I get stuck in the trance-like state of 'not enough-ness', it helps me to imagine that I am one jigsaw piece, and others are different jigsaw pieces. Together, we can create a beautiful picture, and even, a whole new world.

Engagement Practice: Roles

Below are some guiding questions that you can use to engage with the image above. Write down the answers in your journal and use them as a source of reflection.

1. What do you notice?
2. What values call to you? Circle the ones in the middle of the visual that connect with you or add others. When do you feel most aligned with these values?
3. What are you seeking to change? Is it a system of power, a mindset, or a policy? You can also choose to write on a particular issue, campaign, or crisis that calls to you to take action.
4. Locate yourself on the visual and put your name inside the circles that you find yourself playing most frequently. Add other circles if you need and label them with roles (not job titles). Recognise that you can play multiple roles, and that these roles can shift depending on the context. Write the roles below and identify their characteristics (check the definitions for ideas).

5. What role(s) do you feel comfortable and natural playing, and why? What role(s) make you come alive, and why? Are there any differences between these two responses that you can explore? Reflect on how your roles embody the values you identified earlier.
6. What role(s) are you often asked to step into by others? How do you feel about assuming those roles?
7. What is the impact of playing these roles on you - physically, energetically, emotionally, or spiritually? What/who sustains you?
8. In your role(s), how often do you vision and dream? What is the effect of repetition and redundancy, or compromise and sacrifice, in the roles you play?
9. How does your role connect to your privilege and power? For example, are there roles where you might be taking too much space (or not enough)?
10. What story emerges about you when you review the visual and your reflections?
11. How could you stretch yourself? Where can you take bolder risks?
12. When (and not if) you make mistakes, how do you acknowledge them, and course correct without feeling like you've failed?

If you are working in an organisation, Deepa Iyer reminds us how useful it can be to answer these questions with an eye towards understanding and assessing how your organisation functions as part of a campaign, coalition, network, or ecosystem, and how you can course correct to deepen your impact.

Non-Violent Communication

Changemakers and activists, particularly those who find themselves in situations of importance and urgency, often end up emotionally triggered, and then communicate in ways that hurt or harm. The very challenges they're trying to resolve in the outside world, seem to happen within the NGO, or school, or spiritual community.

These unskilful interactions damage those involved, and the relationship in between. By learning interpersonal mindfulness, we can communicate our needs more accurately, while also listening deeply to the needs of others. These techniques allow us to cultivate valuable relational skills of empathy, compassion, and a better understanding of self and other.

> *"When we are busy judging people,*
> *we have no time to love them."*
> ~ Dr Marshall Rosenberg

Marshall Rosenburg, an American psychologist, mediator, author, and teacher, developed invaluable work in the field of Non-Violent Communication. A simple, 4-step process, his methods ask us to take full responsibility for what we are thinking and feeling, before making a request for our needs to be met by others. It seems straightforward, but it doesn't mean that it's easy. The process provides useful guidelines, whether we are reflecting on our own behaviour, or in the context of a relationship with another.

Here are the steps:

1. Observe what is happening, without judgement – this is an invitation to stop the 'who's right, who's wrong' game and cultivate skills of direct seeing.
2. Identify how you are feeling – not just the presenting emotion, but any other emotions that you believe to be less socially acceptable, such as jealousy, or shame, or anger.
3. Identify your needs – what would make life more wonderful for you in this moment? You may find that you can meet your own needs, or you may need to request that your needs be met by another. If this is the case, you will need to include step 4.
4. Make a request – not a demand, but a request. Ask in such a way that the other can meet your need, or negotiate a different way of meeting your need, which feels authentic for them.

> ### Contemplative Practice: NVC with Yourself
>
> Sit in meditation and see if you can identify what you are experiencing in the moment. If you are feeling relaxed and at ease, savour the experience, allowing it to nourish you.
>
> If you are feeling any unpleasant or aggravating experiences, or if a difficult memory comes up, then go through the four steps. If the memory involves a disagreement with another person, imagine making a request to them that could help you meet your need. Alternatively, make a request to yourself.
>
> For this practice, there is no need to engage with another. Simply practice the steps and reflect on how this changes your relationship with the uncomfortable experience.

Many of us did not develop a language for feelings when we were growing up. We often think our feelings, instead of experiencing them.

In Appendix B at the back of this book, I've included lists of universal human needs, and the feelings that can arise when these needs are met or not met. It can be helpful to read through these lists regularly as you learn to identify your feelings and needs, in order to develop a broader repertoire of feelings- and needs-related language.

> ### Shadow Integration Practice: Reflective Journaling
>
> Use your journal as a place to explore a difficulty that arose for you this week.
>
> A private journal can be a safe space to investigate your own biases and judgements, which tend to create conflict with others.
>
> You might want to try following these steps:
>
> 1. In neutral language, write down what you observed about the difficult situation. What actually happened?
> 2. Next, explore how you felt. What difficult emotions came up for you? Use the appendix if you find it hard to identify emotions.
> 3. What were your needs in that moment? We all have basic human needs for respect, safety, appreciation, understanding, support, etc. See if you can write these down without judging yourself unkindly.
> 4. Finally, imagine making a request to the person that would help resolve the situation. Remember that it is a request, not a demand. How would you word it?

HOME PRACTICES

1. Individual contemplative practices are important to prime our awareness of other beings. It is through our connectedness, and our willingness to show solidarity with others, that social change can take place. Keeping this focus on the connections within ecosystems, you can journal on these prompts, which are also from from Deepa Iyer's work:

- Who are you connected to? What roles do they play? Start with your immediate ecosystem (usually your organisation), and then zoom out to include mentors, supporters, co-conspirators, friends, and colleagues, outside of your organisation.
- The middle circle in the visual identifies the values of the communities and the world we seek to create. Which of these resonate with your ecosystem and why? How does your ecosystem create the conditions for justice, liberation, solidarity, and inclusion to be realised?

- What observations emerge about your team, organisation, network, or movement, when you review the complete ecosystem, and your role within it?
- An effective, healthy, and sustainable social change ecosystem requires people to play diverse roles. Is your map imbalanced in any way? If so, how could the ecosystem provide support, alter objectives, or course correct?
- Often, social change ecosystems are prone to maintaining cultures of overwork, productivity, and performance, at the cost of individual wellbeing and long-term sustainability. Does the mapping process provide insights into the culture of your ecosystem? Are there roles that need to be strengthened to cultivate a more sustainable culture?

2. Another worthwhile practice is to use your mealtimes as a practice of mindfulness. Each meal can become a chance to touch into the truth of interconnectedness. Recite this food blessing before you eat and see how it changes your relationship to the meal.

*"This food is the gift of the whole universe, the Earth, the sky,
and much hard work.
May we eat in such a way as to be worthy to receive it.
May we transform our unskilful states of mind and learn to eat in moderation.
May we take only food that nourishes us and prevents illness.
We accept this food in order to realise the path of understanding and love."*
~ Thich Nhat Hanh

CHAPTER 4
Our Indestructible Essence

*"Look at the sun. The sun is shining.
Nobody polishes the sun. The sun just shines.
We don't have to try too hard
to find ourselves.
We haven't really lost anything;
we just have to tune in."*
~ Chögyam Trungpa

Many spiritual traditions believe that we all have an indestructible essence, a wellspring of goodness in our hearts that is innate to all living beings. It is a quality of wakefulness and witnessing that expresses itself as gentleness and warmth. Just being ourselves is enough to bring this goodness into the world.

Different traditions use terms such as Christ Consciousness (Christianity), the Spark of God (Quakers) or Buddha Nature (Buddhism), or in Southern Africa, it is someone with ubuntu (humanity). The name doesn't matter as much as the idea that all of us have goodness within, even if it is temporarily hidden from view.

When we experience difficult moments in life, we often need to self-protect, and we tend to put on armour. This process is important during the time of challenge, but we must not forget our potential for re-opening, and re-connecting, with the people and the world around us. These layers of protection might hide our indestructible essence temporarily, but it is always there.

With this in mind, there's also no need to indulge our suffering. Everyone faces challenges, whatever their circumstances or level of income. We can accept that painful experiences are part of the human condition. It doesn't mean that we are failing or coping badly with life. It is just how it is – some moments bring delight and wonder, and some bring deep despair. Through our own suffering, we can learn to open our hearts to the great well of compassion that resides within each one of us, which makes us more tender and aware of the difficulties of others as well.

You can start to live and meditate with the joy of getting to know yourself at an intimate level. In a way, it is like having a love affair with yourself. Rob Nairn, my first mindfulness teacher, offered teachings on, "the ability to sit in our own unique mess with an open heart and say - this is me; this is where I am, and this is okay. I'm allowed to be me; I do not have to become someone else."

We do not need to perfect ourselves. We can start with ourselves, just as we are.

Jack Kornfield, the author, and Buddhist practitioner, reminds us that we are already whole and our daily meditation practice does not need to be a grim duty of self-improvement. You can focus your attention on flourishing; on using your talents to bring joy, both to yourself and to others. You are unique and must trust that you have something to offer. The work you need to do is simply to perfect your ability to listen, and to love.

> **Contemplative Practice: Already Whole**
>
> Find a comfortable way to sit on a chair, or on the floor, and allow your spine to lengthen. Notice the points of contact with the earth, and let gravity settle you, so that there is an increasing sense of connection with the ground beneath you.
>
> See if it feels comfortable to deepen your breathing gently, noticing the physical sensations linked to your inhale and exhale.
>
> Now see if you can connect with any wholesome or positive emotions that are already present, without fabricating anything. Allow yourself the chance to savour them, as if you are shining a warm light on those aspects of yourself.
>
> Bask for a while in whatever supportive experience arises, resourcing yourself for the day that lies ahead. If nothing wholesome seems to be present, rest in the knowledge that you are still breathing, and become more aware of this life-sustaining action.

The Goodness in Others

> *"The first duty of love is to listen."*
> *~ Paul Tillich*

When we are with someone who is aware and kind, it can feel like basking in the sun. Their essence shines through and makes us feel safe and seen. Perhaps someone like this comes to mind as you read these words. Take a moment to relax into that memory and the feeling of connection.

Each of us can be like this for others. It takes a clear intention and a consistent practice, but is possible because it is about recollecting who we already are. It is like seeing the sun re-emerge from behind the clouds.

When you cultivate your own positive qualities, it is easier to recognise those good qualities in others around us. We can water these qualities in ourselves and in others. The more we, as friends, parents, teachers, or mentors, focus on positive qualities, the more the people in our circle of care will notice their own. They may even be able to cultivate them more. If we put a spotlight on their negative qualities, they will grow into those, too!

We need to remember to focus on what is strong, not on what is wrong.

Engagement Practice: Contemplative Dyads

To connect more with your inner goodness, and your ability to use it in support of others, you can work in pairs. Choose a partner you feel comfortable with, in person, on the phone, or online. Explain the practice before you begin:

- Partner A will ask a question, and Partner B will answer it.
- Then Partner A says, "Thank you," and asks the question again.
- Repeat the question until the timer runs out – three minutes is usually long enough.
- Partner A then reflects on what they heard. This can help to deepen the sense of being seen and understood, which is integral to relationship building or repairing.
- After a moment of stillness and silence, switch roles.

It is not back-and-forth asking, you answer/ask the same question repeatedly. The role of the listener is simply to listen, with their whole body, to the person who is speaking. There is no need to think of a useful response or to ask questions. As a listener, you're just giving your full attention to the other person.

Questions to Experiment with:
- Tell me something I don't already know about you.
- What wholesome or positive experiences are you feeling right now?
- What have you been grateful for this week?
- What brings you joy?

After the dyad practice, reflect on the experience in your journal or with your partner.
- Note any physical sensations, feelings, or thoughts, that arose within you, while you were listening.
- Note any physical sensations, feelings, or thoughts, that arose within you, while you were speaking.
- Describe the relationship between you before, and after, doing the practice.

> - How did it feel for you to listen without having to think of an answer? Is this usual for you, or does it differ to your usual communication style?
> - If you contemplated the question on gratitude or joy, notice whether your experiences were related to the material world, the natural world, or relationships.

Small, Broad, Vast Mind

*"The mind is not inside the body.
The body, the mountain, everything, is inside the mind."*
~ Dogen

Very often, I forget my indestructible essence and get stuck in my small, narrow mind. The small mind is the one that wants everything to be just a little bit different; when I am with others, I want to be alone, and when I am alone, I want company. I often want to control the external world; a tweak here, an adjustment there, or a complete global makeover. The small mind is either grasping for what it thinks would make it happier or rejecting what it is currently experiencing.

When I'm enjoying a moment of relaxation, this small mind of mine starts chirping that I should be doing something more useful. When I'm feeling dispirited or depressed, my small mind catastrophises, telling me that these feelings may never end. It is tricksy and troublesome, yet it seems to be my default mode when I am not conscious or aspiring to something more meaningful.

The small mind can sometimes acknowledge the needs of close family and friends, but it is dominated by the imperative to ensure that the self feels safe and secure. This is often called the reptilian brain, with its sole mandate for survival. We need to eat, to protect ourselves, and our families, and to ensure the next generation of the species continues. The author, Karen Armstrong, calls this the Four Fs: feeding, fighting, fleeing, and f… reproducing. The small mind has a role to play because it ensures our survival. However, once our basic needs are met, the small mind should not be left in charge. In fact, its narrow-minded approach to life brings little benefit to our long-term happiness, or indeed, to the flourishing of a just society.

Maybe you can think of your small mind as a fractious toddler in the kitchen. You certainly don't want to let that toddler near the knives or the stove because chaos would reign. You also don't want to lock that toddler away in the pantry – it would be cruel and probably cause even more chaos. Why not give that toddler a wooden spoon and a saucepan, and let them bash away, making their own music? That's how to work skilfully with your inner child, too.

When the small, egocentric mind begins to quieten, we also realise that we suffer less. We can train it to stay present and accept what is here, rather than longing for an imagined future, or perpetually regretting a past mistake.

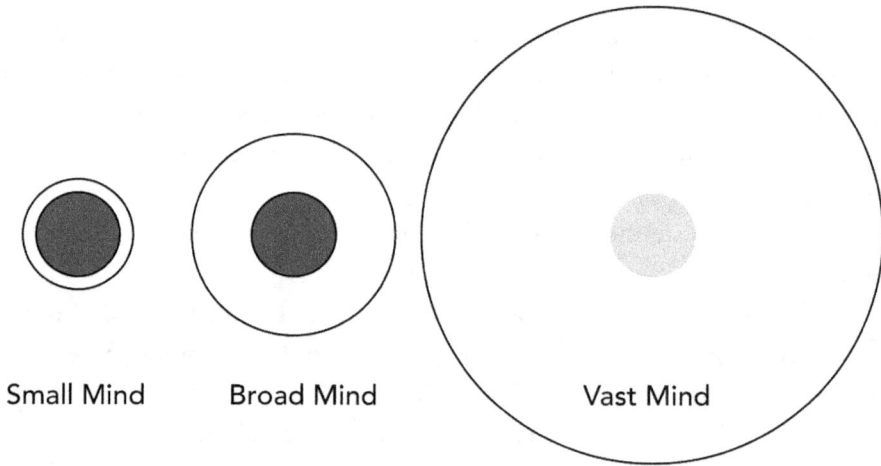

Fig 7. The Mind's Potential

In Figure 7, the inner circle represents the sense of self, our ego-centric focus, while the outer circle is our scope of attention. With the small and broad mind, our sense of self is solid, while the vast mind is still aware of the self, but is more adaptable and less rigid. It has the sense of being in relationship with everything. The scope of attention expands and expands, seeing all beings as equally important as the self. Our own difficulties feel much less problematic once we see them as part of our common human experience.

We can slowly broaden the mind by meeting others from different backgrounds, cultures, and viewpoints. We read, we learn, we explore. A broader, open mind loves difference and adapting to the unpredictable nature of life. It flows more smoothly around obstacles and feels energised to change the things that cause harm but is also able to accept the things it cannot change. The sense of self is still there, we do not disappear, but we seem to expand in our scope, our vision, and our sphere, of care and influence.

My broad mind is much more pleasant company than my small one. It loves others and is keen to learn about their joys and sorrows. It loves travel and adventure and can perceive beauty with vividness. It is appreciative and grateful for the life I have, and it cries for the suffering of others and the potential destruction of the fragile planet that sustains human life.

Sometimes, however, my small mind subtly appropriates my broad mind. It feels that it knows better than others and has the right to judge them. I've found the clarity in this poem very helpful in inspiring the continued call to expand my mind's potential:

"In the beginner's mind there are many possibilities;
in the expert's mind there are few…
In the beginner's mind there is no thought,
'I have attained something.'
All self-centred thoughts limit our vast mind.
When we have no thought of achievement,
no thought of self, we are true beginners.
We can really learn something."
~ Shunryu Suzuki

The expert's mind can be the small mind in disguise, if it maintains a strong egocentric focus. So, let's go bigger, aspiring to greatness, vastness, and expansiveness. The challenge with developing a vast mind seems to be the process of unlearning all that we have studied! To meet each moment with real awareness, we need to put aside our formal training, our hard-earned degrees, and strong opinions, and sense into the embodied wisdom that's yearning to emerge. When we can settle back to trust our indestructible essence, then we have nothing to protect or defend, and we can grow into our vast potential.

Occasionally, we meet someone with a vast mind, or read the words of those who are able to touch on the universal nature of humanity. We may even get glimpses of our own expansiveness when we are with them. This can inspire us to look beyond our selfish needs with the promise that, although paradoxical, we'll become much happier.

It's for reasons such as these that people are willing to travel across continents to meet with spiritual elders like His Holiness the Dalai Lama, Archbishop Desmond Tutu, Amma, the hugging saint, His Holiness the 17th Karmapa, and the Pope. When you are with them, it's possible to touch into a sense of timelessness, and the immeasurable qualities that they embody, such as love, compassion, joy, and equanimity. People feel inspired to participate in the projects or organisations that they set up, even knowing that they may never see the results.

A vast mind spans time zones and generations. This type of person still has a sense of self, and acknowledges the embodied nature of the human mind, yet their vast mind can tap into something much more spacious. It is without boundaries; interconnected with all other minds, throughout space and time. It does not resist external experiences but responds to them with interest. It is content with, and accepting of, life, which unfolds in each moment.

In 2010, I spent a few days in the company of the vast mind of Choje Akong Tulku Rinpoche at the Tara Rokpa Centre in South Africa. He moved slowly, yet with absolute awareness. His instructions were clear and always kind. He laughed with us and spoke about his escape from Tibet. What delighted me was the way that all of us around him seemed to rediscover our kindest selves. We not only wished to be of service but found joy in doing so.

A man (who is now my husband) was up on a hill in the searing summer heat, digging holes to bury some *bompas*, urns that had been empowered to heal the earth. With sweat pouring down his face, he still managed to smile and light a fire for a smoke puja. We all gathered branches of fragrant plants and offered them to the fire. To this day, whenever I walk across that hillside, I feel a sense of the sacred, and I'm reminded of that day.

Despite the death of Akong Rinpoche in 2015, his 1000-year vision lives on in the projects he began in Scotland, Tibet, Southern Africa, and across Europe. He was a quiet man, born in a remote Tibetan village, and once worked as an orderly in a British hospital. Yet he inspired thousands of people to take part in his centres and projects, not by what he said, but by how he was with others.

He empowered the Tara Rokpa Centre to be the healing and therapy centre of Southern Africa. He chose its location, saying that the air, land, and water around the province of Gauteng would soon become so polluted that it would harm its residents. With the centre being 250km from Johannesburg, it was far enough to ensure a healthy environment in which people could come for healing, for practice, and to learn ways to connect with themselves, their communities, and the environment around them.

Trusting in the Goodness of Others

Very often, our challenge as changemakers is to see the indestructible essence in others, especially when their behaviour is causing harm. My favourite bugbear is with politicians, particularly those who claim to be serving their constituents, but who are more strongly motivated to serve themselves.

I've driven through parts of South Africa, a beautiful country, where there is no service provision, where sewerage flows through the streets, and litter piles up on every corner or blows across the veld. There is no employment, no electricity, no safe drinking water. My heart feels squeezed dry, and I am someone simply driving past. I do not live there.

Yet I also know that many politicians and municipal leaders are struggling, too. They have their own challenges with budgets, priorities, and a severe lack of support, not to mention relationship difficulties and bereavement. So, it is vital to keep seeing the potential for goodness in everyone. This allows us to continue working with individuals, and in communities, even when it seems like nothing will change.

If we can look closely and see their inner essence, we can build relationships, even if we do not agree with peoples' words or actions. Deeply entrenched structural issues need multi-level attention. On-going relationships allow for important shifts to happen, in contrast to polarised voices, shouting at each other across a chasm.

Most current political systems perpetuate short term policies. Yet, we exist in a time that requires a vast global vision. Some political leaders advocate openly for short-term self-interest, and many people support them. It is not actually our responsibility to change people whom we consider small-minded, as this serves to reinforce binaries and creates othering. After all, they are the only ones who can change themselves.

However, we can work to expand our own scope of care and attention, and we can support those who are being harmed, and those addressing the harm that short-term political expediency causes in the world. We can make the wish to benefit all beings and focus that intention on small daily acts of kindness and generosity. We can take a global and long-term vision to inform our lives moment-by-moment. It's not easy, of course, but I'm not sure that we really have a choice. Our small mind has got us into the mess of the Anthropocene Epoch. And it's now time for the vast, visionary mind to get us out of it.

By incorporating subtle contemplative practices into your daily life, you can learn to understand situations deeply by listening, even to those viewpoints that you do not agree with. You can then make better decisions on how to intervene in situations that are causing harm.

When we can recognise the broad mind of another, it is a chance to acknowledge that we have access to that vastness within ourselves. Our inner contentment is a superpower, because once we realise how few actual needs we have, no-one can manipulate us. And we can start focusing our attention on those around us.
- Which mind do you choose to live from?
- Which mind will you cultivate today?

Watering Wholesome Seeds

Thich Nhat Hanh taught about the seeds that lie dormant within our unconscious mind (or store consciousness). Some seeds are wholesome, such as love, compassion, and mindfulness, and they make our lives, and the lives of those around us, better if we water them (Figure 8.)

However, we all have afflictive seeds too, or unwholesome tendencies, such as hatred, craving, jealousy, or arrogance. When these rise up into our mind consciousness, we behave in ways that we later regret, as they can damage our relationships.

The good news is that we can learn to hold our afflictive seeds with mindful awareness, and remind ourselves that we developed these tendencies as a survival trait, to protect ourselves. If we keep aware of these

Our Indestructible Essence

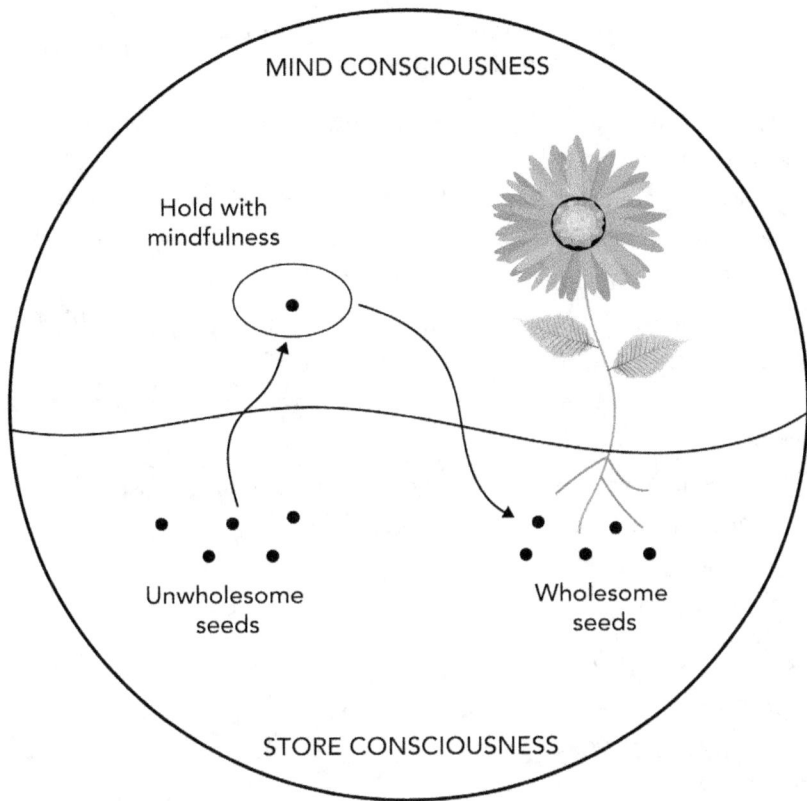

Fig 8. Watering the Seeds of Happiness (Thich Nhat Hanh)

destructive emotions, without acting out on them, we will witness them subside. These are momentary states, and so long as we don't add energy to them, they will dissolve away. Mindfulness becomes a wholesome seed in itself.

With wholesome seeds, we can water them through practices of loving kindness and compassion, so that they grow and flourish, becoming our new habits and traits. This is how mindfulness helps us to lessen our destructive habits and enhances our beneficial traits.

We need to understand destructive tendencies when we are working in social change environments, while maintaining our strength by focusing on the positive qualities that reside in every living being.

Shadow Integration Practice: Unwholesome Qualities

Earlier you undertook a practice to notice some of your wholesome qualities. All of us also have unwholesome qualities within us that cover our true essence. You can attend to these tendencies with mindfulness, acknowledging that they were part of your unconscious conditioning, and that they may have been of great use in the past.

Only after naming them, can you choose whether they are still of use, or whether they can be watered less often, until they disappear of their own accord because your wholesome qualities have grown to fill the space.

Complete five or more of the following sentences, based on your experiences of the past week or month:

I felt angry when…

I was frustrated because…

I realised I was jealous…

I noticed myself desiring more…

I heard myself say, "I hate…" when…

When I compared myself with…, I felt…

I became anxious when…

I was reactive when…

I felt guilty about…

I felt ashamed when…

I felt pity for… because…

I noticed feeling stressed…

What do you notice after doing this exercise? Did you find any recurring patterns that indicate your own shadow? How are your energy levels after writing about these difficult situations? Were your disturbing emotions aroused on behalf of yourself, or others?

"The seeing is the doing."
~ Krishnamurti

Many of us feel exhausted when doing Shadow Integration work because it is not pleasant to gaze at the parts of ourselves that we like to keep hidden. However, when you remember that everyone has less skilful aspects, it can help to ease the burden. It can be reassuring to know that being human means being flawed. You can identify your flaws without shame, and then no one else can hurt you by noticing them.

I remember laughing with a friend who'd been accused of being aggressive. Instead of denying it, she answered, "Yes, it's true, at least I'm not passive aggressive, I'm aggressive aggressive!"

Once the truth of your unskilful tendencies is acknowledged openly, you have a greater chance of finding skilful alternatives.

HOME PRACTICES

1. How are your contemplative practices going? These are the foundation of the course and will help you develop the resilience you need to face everything - the full spectrum of what lies within you, and the whole picture of what lies around you.

2. Which other practices did you do this week and which did you choose to skip? Is it comfortable for you to work in relationship with another person, or do you prefer to work alone? We can learn so much about ourselves when we notice our priorities and our preferences.

> *"It's in the act of having to do things that you don't want to*
> *that you learn something about moving past the self.*
> *Past the ego."*
> ~ bell hooks

CHAPTER 5

The Activist's Achilles

"First, do no harm"
~ Buddhist precept

Activism is the work of transformation. It is messy, relational, and complex, requiring a deep understanding of emotions, as well as theories and facts. This is where we need to take a clear and unflinching look at our shadow as it is revealed through our habitual tendencies, conditioning, bias, and prejudice. We all have shadow material that needs to be brought into the light, so before we can hope to help others, we first need to commit to doing no harm. It is not easy for anyone to see their own unskilfulness and vulnerability, yet this is exactly how we become humble enough to transform the world from the inside out.

In this chapter, we will dive into this boggy terrain and explore four questions: What are the problems, and why do they exist? Which ones are relevant to you? How do we work with them?

While activists may feel that they are motivated by altruism, self-centred tendencies inevitably sneak in – and it is no-one's fault. It is just how we have evolved. We can understand our confusing motivations better by remembering the structure of the triune (or three-in-one) brain. Our brain stem is responsible for our survival and requires motivations linked to safety and sustenance. Within the context of modern, capitalist societies, this then creates a focus on money and status.

Our limbic system, which is the hub of our emotions, is concerned with motivations about connection, love, and belonging. This may mean that we do not challenge harmful actions because our motivation to belong to a group is stronger than our willingness to confront members of that group, even on the issues that we are passionate about.

The prefrontal lobes, unique to human beings, give us the ability to be motivated by a search for meaning and problem-solving. This is where our ethical motivations lie, and the ability to see beyond our own in-group, to act in ways that can heal.

> **Engagement Practice: Needs as Motivation**
>
> Look at the list of Universal Human Needs in the appendix.
>
> Meeting these needs, or honouring these values, is the source of our motivation and multiple motivations can exist simultaneously. Often, we can get confused when they seem to compete.
>
> Identify three of the needs that you seek to meet during your engagement work. Take one from each column (Well-being, Connection, and Self-Expression). Notice whether meeting one need might come into conflict with meeting another. Write about a situation where you experienced this conflict. How did you resolve it?

The Activist's Achilles

You may already be familiar with the story of Achilles. His mother loved him so much that she wanted to make him immortal. As a baby, she held him by his heel and dipped him in the river Styx, which had special powers linked to the Underworld. Her wish was that nothing would be able to harm him. However, the sacred water did not protect the place where she held him and it became his weak spot. He grew up to become one of the greatest Greek warriors and a hero in the Trojan war, but he was still human and eventually, he was killed when an arrow penetrated his heel.

Activists, like everyone, have weak and blind spots, even when working with the intention to help others. There is a difference between impact, and intention, hence the adage, "The road to hell is paved with good intentions."

In reality, the road to heaven may also be paved with good intentions, if we are able to be clear about our motivations, integrate our shadow, and link our innate wisdom with the capacity for altruism.

It can be helpful to explore these tendencies as shadow archetypes, so that we can see our own challenges, biases, and conditioning, from a slightly distanced perspective. These shadow archetypes represent unconscious aspects of our personality that we do not want to see:

- The Wounded Healer
- The Burnout Martyr
- The Controlling Founder
- The White Saviour
- The Razing Firebrand
- The Othering Activist

We'll look at each of these in more detail in the pages that follow to get a clearer sense of our own tendencies. This can feel uncomfortable, so it's important to remember Krishnamurti's advice that, "The seeing is the doing." Once we have seen our own shadow, it can be understood, accepted, and integrated, and this gives us the ability to act more skilfully in the world.

How do we do that? By becoming more aware of our inner world. Reading and accumulating knowledge can certainly help, but contemplation and self-knowledge are even more effective.

Habit Patterns

Our habitual tendencies are deeply entrenched, and they can take a lifetime to re-programme. One way of becoming more familiar with them is to watch the mind with interest and curiosity, rather than judgement or condemnation. It is only once we can witness the movements of our own mind that we can begin to have a choice in terms of how to respond to our inner programming.

You might want to look back at the information about the four movements of the mind, to recall how we get distracted so often. The backtracking practice that follows can be an amusing way of seeing just how swiftly we can get carried away. It is also a helpful way to become familiar with pathways of habit.

> ### Contemplative Practice: Backtracking
>
> Sit comfortably, deepening your breath, or listening to the sounds in your environment. When you find yourself lost in thought, or wanting to shift your position, see if you can trace the movements of your mind backwards. What was the initial stimulus you experienced, such as a sound or a thought? Did you identify it as pleasant, unpleasant, or neutral? Once you did that, what happened next? Did your body want to move, or your mind want to carry on thinking? How long did it take you to realise that you had lost touch with the present moment? Bring yourself back to the breath or sounds and wait until you realise that you are lost once again.

The Wounded Healer

This is one of the classic archetypes identified by psychologist Carl Jung, and it offers insight into the dangers of the shadow, as well as its potential benefits. Jung acknowledged that many in the healing professions are drawn to the work because of their own wounds, often due to adverse childhood experiences. This provides motivation and commitment.

If these personal wounds are not acknowledged, then the healer can suffer or cause harm. If there is an unconscious split between healer and wounded, the healer can develop an inflated ego, acting from a position of superiority, and they may set up a relationship of dependency with the person they're trying to help. They may even project their own wounds onto them, rather than being able to see what would most benefit the person in their care. In addition, these healers can suffer from vicarious trauma and burnout when continually hearing the stories of suffering from their clients, because these stories open their own unhealed wounds.

Once the wounded healer is willing to see deeply into their own issues, great benefits can arise. They develop empathy for the suffering of others and gain insight into its causes. They develop resilience through overcoming their own illnesses or traumas. Wounded healers walk beside their client, holding a safe space for them to find their own healer within. Their own careful self-disclosure can also inspire the client to find hope, and trust their inner healing capacities as well.

The wounded healer tendency is widely recognised, which means that psychologists, counsellors, and all who work with mental health, are required to have supervision from another therapist, where they can explore the difficulties that emerge within themselves. This allows for deepening levels of understanding and skilfulness to develop.

Very few people in the activist world, however, have on-going support and supervision, which is why we need to be more aware of our own shadow material, and be prepared to offer and receive support, from elders or our peers.

The Burnout Martyr

Historically, the term martyr was given to people who suffered, or even killed, for their political or religious beliefs; who were admired for their commitment to the cause. However, their loss of life also meant losing their leadership skills and their insights. In the activist world, martyr syndrome has negative long-term consequences for the individual, their team, and the cause itself. We might shift into this shadow role when we feel that everything relies on us and forget about the community around us.

This overdeveloped sense of responsibility contains two distinct concerns. It means we take away responsibility from those who can take care of themselves, which subtly undermines their capacity to transform and develop resilience. And we neglect to take responsibility for what we need to care for in ourselves, such as our own health. It is the essence of individualism.

This ego-centric focus means that, usually unintentionally, we put ourselves above others, and somehow believe that we can solve all the problems. It sometimes also reflects a lack of trust in others, and in activist work, where our intention is to support peoples' own power and dignity, we can neglect to see their strengths and abilities.

When problems are structural and vast, we need to work with all our collective strengths. It is easy to lose momentum, or to become cynical and bitter, when working in isolation, and this is ultimately counterproductive to the work itself.

Shadow Integration Practice: Investigating the Martyr

Work through the questions below to identify whether the martyr complex might be a tendency of yours. Remember that it is not your fault that it has developed, but once you become aware of it, it is your responsibility to take care and to find alternative ways of relating to your work and the people around you.

- Describe some recent occasions when you have felt overextended, unappreciated, or very angry.
- Write freely about a recent time when you felt a twinge of self-sacrificing resentment.
- Which is the role you most commonly play: victim, persecutor, or rescuer?
- Note down times when you have swooped into the rescue or when you have made do with less than you need.
- Describe moments when you have felt abandoned because no one has noticed your suffering.
- What are the rewards you long for when playing the martyr: appreciation, recognition, or love? Have you ever received these when playing this role?
- Who would you feel safe to talk to about your strong feelings and destructive thoughts?
- How do you feel about self-care? In what ways might self-care feel like self-indulgence to you?
- In what ways do you feel that self-care is a marker of privilege?
- How do you sustain yourself?
- Do you sometimes feel that you need to do everything yourself? If yes, then why?
- What is behind the need to self-sacrifice?
- What was your decision-making like when you last felt exhausted and overwhelmed?
- In what ways can self-care be linked to community-care?

"Caring for myself is not self-indulgence, it is self-preservation, and that is an act of political warfare."
~ Audre Lorde

Empathy fatigue, vicarious trauma, and burnout are symptoms commonly observed in human service professionals, first responders, social change activists, and environmentalists. The cumulative toll is that these individuals often get exhausted, numb, or overwhelmed.

Paul Gorski, an equity and justice educator, author, and speaker, has explored the intersection between martyr syndrome and burnout. The culture of activism can often mean that we negate the need for self-care to put others ahead of ourselves. However, we need to learn skills to keep ourselves healthy and well.

When we are passionate about the work, we are energised. But when things don't move at the pace we want them to, we can lose heart. We can feel as if we cannot go on anymore. Concerningly, when mature activists leave their organisations due to burnout, they take their institutional knowledge with them and this undermines what they could offer to younger activists in terms of sustainability.

Gorski's research also revealed that the main cause of burnout among black racial justice activists was their white colleagues. Our organisations are microcosms of the world we work in, and inevitably, the challenges we confront in the outer world are part of the organisations themselves. This can feel like a betrayal, yet emphasises the point that we need individual transformation before we can hope for social transformation.

Founder and director of The Trauma Stewardship Institute, Laura Lipsky, focuses on how continuous exposure to trauma during social change work can also lead to burnout. She investigates the toll taken on those working to make the world a better place and has experienced how mindfulness practices can be sustaining, allowing for deepening resilience.

Social change agents often feel tired, cynical, or that they can never do enough. These, and other symptoms, affect the individual and the collective. It drains us of the energy we need to benefit humankind, other living things, and the planet. In her book, Trauma Stewardship, Lipsky calls on us all to meet these challenges in an intentional way and to keep overwhelm at bay by developing a quality of mindful presence.

> ### Shadow Integration Practice: Early Warning Signs
> Look through the list below and see which you've experienced in recent years:
> - Lack of sleep
> - Boredom with work
> - Pushing people away
> - Seeking isolation
> - Irritation with people around you
> - Feeling taken advantage of
> - Doubt and questioning
> - Inability to empathise
> - Numbness
> - Shallow breath
> - Sickness and physical pain
> - Feeling busy and distracted
> - Feeling helpless and hopeless
> - A sense that you are not doing enough
>
> Choose five and write down the ways you've been able to support yourself at these times, so that you do not shift into full-blown burnout.

The Controlling Founder

During my life in Southern Africa, I've witnessed many non-profit (NPO) and non-governmental (NGO) organisations go through difficult growth and transition processes, commonly referred to as founder or pioneer syndrome. The founder holds on for many reasons, long after they cease to benefit the organisation. I have no doubt that if I had ever started an NGO myself, I would be writing about my own challenge of relinquishing control.

People and organisations follow similar developmental stages, and the energy, agility, and single-pointed focus that distinguish the early stages of an organisation, can prevent it from maturing into a sustainable and adaptable institution. The person who most wants the organisation to succeed can often be the one that ends up holding it back.

> ### Shadow Integration Practice: Too Controlling?
>
> Whether you're the founder of an organisation, or play a leadership role, have a look through the seven symptoms below (identified by John Greathouse), and see if any of them make you feel uncomfortable. That feeling of unease can be a useful sign that there may be a little shadow following you around.
>
> 1. Do you find it hard to delegate?
> 2. Do you get angry when decisions are made without you?
> 3. Have you felt a sense of paranoia when the organisation seems to be slipping out of your control?
> 4. Have you ever ignored input from subject-matter experts?
> 5. Do you sometimes feel that you can predict what might happen, even though you lack information?
> 6. Do you get irritated with formalised planning and structures?
> 7. Have you side-lined efforts to institute procedures, processes, and controls, that would decentralise decision-making?

A friend, Carly Tanur, writes poignantly about her own experience of founding, growing, and stepping back, from an organisation in Cape Town. She explores by asking the question, "What goes into building more sustainable practices – questioning whether the way we work enables others to take the lead in their lives, or whether we work in ways that ensure that we remain needed? How does doing too much and consistently being too busy impact the quality of the relationships we build, the observations we make, and therefore, the meaning we make of the role we play in bringing about change and transformation?" (Tanur, 2015).

Through critical self-reflection, she was able to shift her leadership practice so that she could create an organisational life that stimulated, enlivened, and deepened the work, while remaining attentive to the wellbeing of the team and the sense of genuine care that was felt within the organisation. The concept that supported her self-reflection was that of 'Anavah', a Hebrew term which suggests that to be humble, is to "occupy a rightful space, neither too much, nor too little" (Morinis, 2007).

By developing a practice of self-reflection, she encouraged herself and her colleagues to take up their rightful space, to step up when necessary, and step back when appropriate. She was able to describe how building this kind of practice was essential, "so that we can work intentionally, responsibly and in ways that are regenerative, for the people we work with, and for us as practitioners."

Letting an organisation go is much like letting a child grow up; it takes courage on the side of the founder, and on the side of those taking over. Self-awareness through reflective practice is what gives everyone the strength this process requires.

The White Saviour

White saviourism is a concept used to describe white people (often from the Global North) who believe they are helping black, indigenous, or people of colour (BIPOC). They may be well intentioned, but their actions tend to perpetuate the inequalities that already exist in society, and undermine the agency of the people they're seeking to serve. In the film industry, the white saviour trope reinforces the message that a white person is needed as the agent of change, or to rescue people of colour from their plight.

This has been the most disturbing shadow archetype for me to explore. I've wondered, is it what brought me to Africa in the first place? Was I influenced by films and the romantic notion of saving others? Am I guilty of this still, I ask, when helping at the soup kitchen in downtown Johannesburg? It is helpful to look back with a compassionate gaze at the person I was before, while maintaining a critically explorative observation of the person I am now, and the initiatives in which I participate.

Living in South Africa, I've felt the necessity and urgency of understanding my own complicity in the systems that hold white privilege in place. In 2018 and 2019, I dived into this work with a willingness to learn and feel discomfort. I eagerly soaked up teachings on race by Doris Chang, john a. powell, and Zenju Earthlyn Manuel at the Mind & Life summer school in New York State, and from Ruth King and Rhonda Magee at a Mindfulness Conference in South Africa. I read Resma Menaken's book on anti-racism, watched YouTube videos on white fragility by Robin DiAngelo, and devoured essays on liberatory practices by bell hooks. I did what academics do – researched and read, hoping that I would be able to put the learnings into practice, without messing it up.

At this time, I was offering a course on Critical Reflexive Praxis for arts activists, and I was warned that it would be a cauldron for discomfort, projection, and vulnerability. It did not disappoint. I got to explore many of my own areas of conditioning and lack of understanding, and the students challenged me and each other about theirs, too. We were frequently uncomfortable, and struggled through together, trying to offer support to each other from our own woundedness, and stay with our compassionate, but critical reflexivity.

Critical Race Theory originated in the United States and trainers in Diversity, Equity and Inclusion suggest working in racial affinity groups to explore unconsciously held beliefs about race. This is intended to give space for each racial community to tell their own stories and do their own work without people of colour having to do the emotional labour or being triggered by the lack of awareness of their white colleagues. Creating safe spaces can allow a deeper awareness before returning to work in diverse racial groups.

South Africa is different, though, and despite my best intentions, as a non-South African, it's been hard for me to sense into the nuanced sources of pain. Rather than holding open a sharing circle, I looked for ways to offer solutions from all that I had read and learned. As trainee drama therapists, the students didn't need solutions, and they were willing to stay together and explore issues face-to-face. They moved me deeply with the saying, "It does not matter who you are, it matters how you are."

This racially diverse group of students demonstrated for me where critical theory falls short in the South African context, and I was drawn to the insights of the late university lecturer, Kennedy Chinyowa. He has written about "the inherent complexities that are hidden in contradictory situations of oppression", such as black people collaborating with the apartheid system; white people acting as allies during the liberation struggle; black people falling into reverse racism after the struggle; and the pervasive presence of the 'oppressor' within the 'oppressed' taking the form of gender-based violence (Chinyowa, 2022).

This experience gave me a clear understanding of the difference between knowledge and wisdom. Knowledge is in the head; wisdom comes from the heart and the body. I experienced how there are no quick solutions to these unconscious biases; there is mess and complexity, both of which we need to be able to hold.

How, then, can white saviours explore this shadow tendency skilfully? In what ways can we challenge what Teju Cole has called the 'White-Savior Industrial Complex', which has roots in Western imperialism? Suggestions include learning to stay present with discomfort, acknowledging deep structural issues, avoiding the performative tendency of 'good whiteness', and being willing to be held accountable.

White saviours try to soothe their own emotional discomfort by carrying out individual acts of kindness, instead of challenging the structures on which inequalities are based. Nicky Falkof, a South African academic who eloquently explores the performative nature of being 'a good white', describes it as, "A politics of pity that is concerned with the goodness of the giver, rather than the historical and structural conditions that underlie the inequality." She quotes Markus Balkenhol, who describes "Whites as the rescuers, saviours of blacks, driven by pity and compassion, rather than solidarity or justice."

Understanding the privilege and power dynamics that underlie the historical inequities between the Global North and South could help us forge new relationships. Much benefit could come from cooperation across hemispheres and borders when facing humanitarian struggles. But those in positions of privilege need to work to amplify and support, not overpower, patronise, or perform compassion.

> *"If you have come to help me, you are wasting your time.*
> *But if you have come because your liberation*
> *is bound up with mine, then let us work together."*
> *~ Lilla Watson and the Aboriginal activists' group,*
> *Queensland, 1970s*

White saviours tend to think of themselves as experts and act as individuals, so Danielle Taana Smith advises: "You need to be willing to not be at the centre of the work or the solution and to follow the advice, expertise, and request of the people who are closest to the pain and the problem." Instead of working as an individual, it is better to work through a reflective organisation where you can be held accountable for your privilege.

> ## Shadow Integration Practice: The White Saviour
>
> What feelings arise for you as you read the section above on the white saviour complex?
>
> Have you ever experienced the impulse to jump in and help in a situation without learning the background story? If you gave in to that impulse, what was the result?
>
> If you are a person of colour, do you find resonance in the description of white people coming to the rescue, and did they show the need to perform these good acts?
>
> When have you (or your communities) been the recipient(s) of such efforts?
>
> What are some ways that we might avoid the pitfalls of sentimentality when trying to act against injustice?

If you are white and you feel ready to reflect on, and confront, some of the unexplored aspects of your racial identity and the privilege that comes with it, there are many excellent books (mentioned in the references) and online courses on anti-racism. Just remember that putting these insights into action will inevitably be accompanied by discomfort. However, white fragility is no longer an option. Not if we wish to heal racial divisions and address what Ruth King calls 'a heart disease' (King, 2018).

When I was working with a South African healer, Zola Xashimba, he commented that, "White people need to come to Africa to heal." This was such an illuminating statement for me, because it highlighted my own experience. It is through living on this continent that I've found healing from the individualism and materialism of the Global North, and a felt sense of common humanity. I have 'saved' no-one in my time here, and I am not even sure I can save myself. But I intend to keep trusting in my indestructible essence, with the wish to combine compassion with the penetrating wisdom needed to unravel biased perception.

The Razing Firebrand

One of the reasons I've heard that (mainly white) people feel uncomfortable around the word "activist" is the association of the term with aggression, hatred, anger, or violence. However, this is not the root of the word. It comes from the Latin 'actus', which is 'a doing, a driving force, or an impulse' and it was first used in early 1900s in the context of anti-war activism.

Destructive protests, when buildings are burnt or lives lost, tend to make headline news, and can overshadow and undermine the arduous work of the committed activist. Nevertheless, it is necessary to explore the anger that can underlie activism, and how it can be used effectively.

Anger is both a friend and a foe of activists. It provides the fire and energy for the difficult work of social, racial, or climate justice, but it can also do harm. It is the energy for the crucible that transforms metal into gold. We need to stay outraged by injustice, while staying sane and capable of working collaboratively. Anger is a life-preserving emotion and an evolutionary response to threat. It lets us know that boundaries have been crossed, or that harm is being caused to the self or others we care about.

Uncontained anger can move in two directions, inwards or outwards, both of which can cause on-going harm. Inward turning anger can bring forth self-blame, where we berate ourselves for something that is often out of our direct control, or it becomes passive aggressive through cynicism or disengagement. These are enemies of the activist, as our effectiveness comes through sensing into the causes of harm and finding the underlying issues that need to be addressed through skilful action or skilful speech.

Alternatively, anger turns outwards and causes us to act or speak in ways that perpetuate retaliation. We project onto others and their threat systems can be triggered, making them project back. This cycle is never-ending, as we see in so many situations of intergenerational violence, where later generations do not even know the original cause of the conflict. They have been conditioned to hate another group unquestioningly, without understanding the original place of harm.

"Stay outraged without losing your mind."
~ Charlene Carruthers

Anger is a powerful fuel for the activist and needs careful navigation. It can be aroused by compassion and altruism, and it can be aroused by hatred. There is a difference between anger that's fuelled by biased perception, and anger that results in clear, forceful action directed against injustice or evil.

How can we differentiate between the two?

One form of anger is moral outrage, which can mobilise grand actions that rectify injustices. Moral outrage means that leaders at community or national levels can transform the overpowering experience of anger into effective action. Yet this occurs only if we are able to mobilise the energy of moral outrage in the service of compassion. Fierce compassion is the energy of the mother whose children are in danger. She is swift and clear, and once the danger has passed, she returns to tranquillity and a sense of loving care. Fierce compassion has no residue in the way that anger or hatred tends to.

When harm is taking place, it requires skilful action. This is where the subtle activism of mindfulness can be so vitally important, as it gives us a tiny gap between the stimulus or experience that triggered the arising of anger, and our response. It is the gap that allows our prefrontal cortex to regulate our threat-focused amygdala. Once the motivation behind our work is clear, it becomes easier to work sustainably and skilfully, remembering the imperative to "First, do no harm".

When anger is the primary driver, and is not contained within the hearth of community and care, we burn others or burn out. The emotional nature of the work often means that activists struggle with relationships. When dealing with vast structural issues that seem impossible to solve, there can be deep feelings of powerlessness, and activists become susceptible to anxiety and stress, outrage, and numbness.

Shadow Integration Practice: Investigating Anger

Think of a time in the last few weeks, when you've experienced anger. Describe the situation in your journal.

- What was your pre-existing mood at the time?
- Who, or what, was the object of your anger?
- How did it feel in your body?
- Were you able to differentiate between the behaviour of the person that triggered your anger, and the person themselves?
- How would your anger change if you realised that they were acting out of ignorance, as opposed to acting on purpose to cause harm?

- When your anger was aroused, who seemed to be in the position of power – you or the object of your anger?
- What does moral outrage mean to you? Was there a sense of this within your experience of anger?
- What does fierce compassion mean to you? If your anger was rooted in compassion, how could you respond to the situation in a way that differs from responding with hatred or rage?

The Othering Activist

Othering is grounded in a sense of duality: us versus them. Whether we are othering from the belief that another group is acting against the common good, or due to our self-centred desires, it creates separation and needs to be explored carefully.

Othering appears to be an evolutionary mechanism, where we prioritise the needs of our in-group (such as family, friends, or like-minded community) over the needs of an out-group. Without awareness, we find ourselves on two sides of a gaping chasm and can find no bridge across.

> "When we see others as the enemy, we risk becoming what we hate.
> When we oppress others, we end up oppressing ourselves.
> All of our humanity is dependent upon recognising the humanity in others."
> ~ Archbishop Desmond Tutu

As South African activist, Nirmala Nair, has written: "By its very nature, activism creates a tension - a polarised tension, a dichotomy, of two opposing camps - us and them. These camps are like two groups of protagonists: those who are on the right track and those who are not. A varied spectrum of activities ensues - holding this tension; moving with it; never letting it sag; and never releasing it. Therein lies the continuation of the struggle. For many, this has become a way of life, and a collapsing of this tension means collapsing identities, collapsing boundaries. Often the waters of struggle become deep and murky, stale, and stagnant. The same voices echo. The same forces become stumbling blocks preventing creative regeneration. Often the activist terrain becomes the playground to enact, externalise, and act out, the inner polarities and unprocessed tensions."

john a powell, from the Haas Institute, speaks of othering as the problem of the 21st Century. As countries have become more diverse, people appear to have become more anxious. Anxiety is a natural response to change and is neither good nor bad; it just points to a need for safety and belonging. We tend to address anxiety in two different ways, through bonding or bridging. It is the difference between these responses that makes or breaks communities.

Bonding implies identifying with your in-group because of the fear of others. There is a sense that someone must lose if others are winning. Each group is defined in opposition to the other. Bridging allows for a sense of belonging across groups, through the cultivation of empathy and understanding. As powell says, "When we bridge, we not only open up to others, we also open up to change in ourselves – and actively participate in co-creating a society to which we can all belong."

Shadow Integration Practice: Othering

Here are some signs of othering. Notice if you've done any in the last week, as othering can be very subtle. It involves unconscious assumptions about others, making it very hard to spot without a time of reflection.

- Attributing positive qualities to people who are like you and negative qualities to people who are different.
- Believing that people who are different from you or your social group pose a threat to you or your way of life.
- Feeling distrustful or upset with people of a social group, even though you don't know anyone from that group.
- Refusing to interact with people because they are different from you and your social group.
- Thinking that people outside your social group are not as intelligent, as skilled, or as special as you and your group.
- Thinking of people only in terms of their relationship with specific social groups, without giving any thought to them as individuals.

We all do this at some level, even when we feel we are defending the rights of others against harm. Most of us are not even aware that we are othering because bias is very hard to identify. Othering then becomes an invisible barrier that separates one group from another: insiders versus outsiders.

> ### Contemplative Practice:
> ### Aspiring, Dissolving and Equalising
>
> Bring to mind someone you find difficult or for whom you have little regard. Imagine that this person is in front of you and focus on the felt sense of their presence. Start by aspiring to be kind, even if it feels challenging. Imagine that they are facing suffering and the reason they are difficult is because they are struggling in some way. See if you can direct words of kindness towards them, such as:
>
> - May you be well and happy.
> - May you be free from pain and suffering.
> - May you experience joy and well-being.
>
> Notice how you feel when you wish them well. Does your heart feel contracted, or is it possible to sense into some tenderness? Notice what is arising for you - there is no right or wrong way to feel, and you do not need to force anything.
>
> Next, try to dissolve your fixed perception of them. Shift your perspective and try to see your adversary in a different light, perhaps the way their child or close friend might see them. Reflect that your feelings are to do with you and your relationship with them - it is nothing intrinsic within them. This does not mean that you must condone their negative or harmful actions.
>
> Finally, reflect that just like you, this person wants to be happy, and just like you, this person wants to be free from suffering. They do not want to be disliked or criticised. See if you can let the humanity of this person touch you, by remembering their indestructible human essence. Despite your differences, there is more that connects you, than separates you. We are all the same in wanting to find happiness.
>
> At the end of this practice, allow the image of this person to fade and spend a few moments tuning into the feelings that may have arisen within your body. Bring some compassion to yourself if difficult feelings are present.

How to Integrate the Shadow

> *"The key instruction is to stay in the present.*
> *Don't get caught up in the hopes of what you might achieve*
> *and how good your situation will be some day.*
> *What you do right now is what matters."*
> ~ Pema Chodron

During our meditation practices, we're aware that thoughts and feelings arise spontaneously and there is nothing we can do to stop them. Even if the thoughts are unkind or hateful, they are not our fault; they are a product of our fears, needs and conditioning. Once we are aware of the thoughts and feelings, then we have the responsibility to work with them as honestly as possible. We can also notice how they shift and change, depending on the circumstances.

Being more mindful can be uncomfortable at first, as we become more and more aware of our unwholesome habitual tendencies, such as biases and prejudice. Don't give up. These become the opportunities for our personal transformation. We become aware of our habits, and gain the presence of mind to respond to them differently.

Once we can see what needs to transform in ourselves, we can bring greater understanding and patience into our work for social transformation and healing. If it is hard for you to change, you will better be able to recognise how hard it is for everyone else. You might make the mistake of thinking that you and others have a fixed identity, but this simply isn't true. Peoples' views and behaviours may seem solid and intransigent, but they can change swiftly, or over time, depending on the circumstances.

Perhaps the most beneficial aspect of cultivating a mindfulness practice is that we learn to sit with discomfort and complexity. This is vital, as we unravel the deep and often intergenerational conditioning of biases and prejudice. As a white person, I've found it necessary to sit in the profound discomfort of recognising the harm caused by colonisation, apartheid, and all forms of racialised oppression that continue today. Sitting quietly as witness builds resilience and heals fragility. As a woman, I have witnessed, and felt personally, how gender-based oppression causes terrible harm and undermines the potential of the world's majority.

Without facing these truths, there's little we can do to address the underlying structures that hold oppression in place.

> ### Contemplative Practice: No Self
>
> Use a timer for 3 - 4 minutes, and write freely using the prompt: "I am..."
>
> Allow anything that comes to mind to find its way onto the page – your roles, your personality traits, your names, relationships with others, etc. Don't edit or censor yourself in any way.
>
> Once the time is up, have a look through the list, and count how many different aspects you've identified. Are you a single self or a multiplicity of different aspects?
>
> Next, with a highlighter pen, or an identifying mark, see how many of these identities put you in relationship with others e.g., son, daughter, wife, cousin, boss, etc. Are you an independent self or interdependent? Does your identity rely on the existence of others?
>
> Finally, have a look through the list, and with a different highlighter pen, see how many of those aspects change moment to moment, or over time, or are permanent? Are we solid and fixed, or ever-changing?

This exercise is intended to give you a sense of the truth that we are not a singular, permanent, or independent self. Rather, we contain a multiplicity of selves, which are ever-changing and interconnected with others. This can offer us a sense of spaciousness when difficult situations arise. It also means that we can trust in the truth that everyone changes, even if we don't like what they do, or the views that they hold. Everything is fluid and flexible if we give it enough attention. Everything can change, even in the direction of justice, solidarity, and compassion.

At this point, we end where we began, circling back to Maclean's work on the triune brain. He offers us hope by identifying the human potential contained within our distinctive brain structure: "Unique to humans, abilities such as foresight and insight merge to create empathy and altruism, where the boundaries between the well-being of self and others start to fade and become dependent on one another."

HOME PRACTICES

Having examined the shadow archetypes, reflect on the following questions.
- Which one or two apply most strongly to you?
- What did you discover about yourself?
- What strengths could you gain by learning to navigate these potential weaknesses?
- How could you find inner resilience by transforming the early warning signs of burnout?

CHAPTER 6

The Activist Archetype

*"Warriors do not win victories by
beating their heads against walls,
but by overtaking the walls.
Warriors jump over walls;
they don't demolish them."*
~ Carlos Castaneda

    The concept of the spiritual warrior or compassionate activist is not a new one. Many wisdom traditions revere those who transcend their egocentric desires. By jumping over the walls of ignorance, they find their true purpose, which is to be of service to others.

    These are the spiritual warriors who become so attuned to the present moment that they know how to attend to others' short- and long-term needs. In Buddhist teachings, this archetype is known as the bodhisattva. The name refers to someone who has great compassion for all living beings and a deep wish to awaken fully to be of service to them. Bodhisattvas become enlightened through taming, and then training, their own minds to act wisely in the world. Once their mind is free from negative and conflicting emotions, they are unafraid to love.

It is this love that motivates action.

Bodhisattvas personify the compassionate, healing, and regenerative drive of thriving natural systems. A simple change in one part of the system allows a cascade of positive results because a skilful action in a particular moment can change the course of human history. A bodhisattva embodies the evolution of humanity, from violence to wisdom, from cruelty to care, and from oppression to social justice.

For an aspiring bodhisattva-in-training, like you and me, there is no expectation that we must be perfect. Rather, that we wish to transform our unskilful qualities in the direction of wisdom and compassion. Wisdom refers to the realisation that we are not separate from the world around us; that we are deeply interconnected. Compassion puts this realisation into practice by acting for the benefit of all.

We cultivate a bodhisattva intention, while still recognising that we are doing the best we can within this body, and with the talents we've inherited from our ancestors. A useful check-in is to keep asking yourself, "What can I do to make this situation better?"

Spiritual warriors are willing to help where help is needed, yet they do not interfere with someone else's need to learn life lessons through difficult experiences. They do not take away the agency of others. They seem to embody paradoxical qualities, such as ease and swift action, compassion and ferocity. This fierce compassion is never carried out with ill will. Rather, it helps cut through ignorance and delusion when someone is causing harm to themselves or others. The bodhisattva focuses on the harmful action, without negating the humanity of the one who is causing harm.

Spiritual warriors know how to attend to their own basic needs, so that they are sustainable, and they can strategize for the long term. The work of the spiritual warrior is sometimes adversarial, yet it also involves seeing deeply into the causes of difficulty, rather than just blaming others for their harmful behaviour.

When we act well, without attachment to the fruits of our actions, we can find joy and value in the work itself. Our role might just be to build the foundation in order to pave the way for others to achieve longed-for results. We can never truly know what the results of our actions will be, as there are so many causes and conditions, and we are all interdependent. It's worth remembering that even the smallest beats of the butterfly's wings are said to set great social movements in motion.

> ### Contemplative Practice: Working with Ignorance
>
> Overcoming ignorance is one of the hardest challenges we face. How do we know what we don't know?!
>
> As you practice today, you can work with the insight practices of open monitoring and reflection. After settling down and taking five deep breaths, open your field of awareness to your inner world and the outer world.
>
> Then ask yourself, "What is here? In my thoughts, feelings, and physical sensations?"
>
> Silently note everything that you become aware of – a headache, birdsong, grief, tingling, sirens, smooth breath, an itch, the warm breeze, anxiety, calm, etc.
>
> Instead of saying "I am grieving, I have a headache, I hear a siren, my leg is tingling," simply notice things as they come and go, without adding the 'I' or 'my'. This will help you to stop identifying with them, which is one of the first steps towards releasing ignorance by realising that you are not your thoughts, or feelings, or physical sensations. They are just experiences that move through your embodied mind.

Green Tara

The image of Green Tara always comes to mind when I talk about compassionate activists. I think of her as a Buddhist feminist and feel a natural affinity. When I took refuge as a Buddhist, I was given the name Dechen Yudron, or Turquoise Lady of Great Bliss, and I aspire to grow into that name and get a taste of bliss!

At the Tara Rokpa Centre in South Africa, where I often practice and facilitate retreats, Tara is the unifying energy, taking care of all who visit by overcoming fear. Overall, I feel that Green Tara represents my aspirations as a compassionate activist. Here is her story, adapted from Buddhist texts of the 16th Century.

Once Upon a Time...

Many eons ago, in the land of Multi-Coloured Light, there lived a princess called Wisdom Moon. Daily, she would go to the temple to study and practice. She possessed great faith and showed complete devotion to the Buddha of the era, known as the Drum Sound Buddha.

In front of this Buddha, she took the bodhisattva vow; the promise to bring all those who suffer to liberation. The monks at the temple were delighted with her promise and her commitment but feared that she would not be able to assist many beings, as she was a woman. They prayed for her to be reborn as a man.

She understood their kind-hearted motivation but was not deterred by their prayers. She realised that their conditioning was a symptom of the era when men held all the positions of power. After all, her own father was a king.

However, Wisdom Moon possessed a vast mind that could access ultimate truth and see far into the future. She vowed, "As long as there is still suffering on this earth, I will benefit beings, appearing in a woman's body."

Since the day of her death, Wisdom Moon has been known as Green Tara, and is viewed as a deity or goddess. Although she achieved enlightenment, she vowed to stay on earth to help beings, and she is available to anyone who prays to her, because of her commitment to carry out the bodhisattva vow.

Particularly in Tibet and Nepal, she has come to be known as the mother of liberation. She represents the virtues of enlightened activity, uniting compassion and action. She rests at ease, watching over the world with a compassionate gaze.

When she hears the cries of beings who are suffering, she acts swiftly to alleviate their difficulties. Her skin has a greenish hue, representing the air element in Tibetan Buddhism. She acts with the swiftness of the wind, whenever she sees suffering, like a parent who senses their child is in danger. Her left leg is bent inwards, showing that she is free from destructive emotions, while the right is lifted, ready to jump into action from her place of stillness. With one hand she gives, enabling all who ask for help to access their innate talents and skills. The other hand is held in the refuge mudra, where the thumb and first finger touch to show the union of wisdom and skilful means. She holds the lotus flower, iconic in Buddhism as a metaphor that the mud of our unskillfulness can be transformed to allow the lotus to bloom. The beauty of the lotus flower represents our fully enlightened qualities, which we can use to touch into the joy of being in service to others.

Pic 2. Green Tara Thangka (at the Tara Rokpa Centre

The Practice of Prayer

When I facilitate retreats in South Africa, I meet people from many different spiritual and faith traditions. I have found it useful to bring together two distinct contemplative practices: meditation and prayer.

Prayer could be thought of as requesting support or asking questions, while meditation opens the space to receiving clarity and guidance. Whether you feel you are praying to a higher power, or to your own wisdom mind, it is an act of humility to recognise that we all need support sometimes. The answers can often come at unexpected moments, such as when you are taking a walk or a shower.

In whatever form that feels appropriate for your belief system, prayer can be a powerful spiritual practice. Mother Theresa is known to have said: "I used to pray that God would feed the hungry, or do this or that, but now I pray that he will guide me to do whatever I'm supposed to do. I used to pray for answers, but now I'm praying for strength. I used to believe that prayer changes things, but now I know that prayer changes us, and we change things."

Prayer helps us align with our deepest sense of purpose and gives us the strength to act in ways outside of our comfort zone. You can direct prayerful requests towards anyone or anything that you feel embodies a sense of vastness – your teachers, deities, ancestors, or the earth itself. This depends on your own belief system.

It doesn't matter who you pray to, it is more important to open beyond your egocentric focus, and humbly ask for help and guidance. After praying, open to a quality of multi-sensory listening. This is where inspiration can arise. Notice whether you experience any physical sensation around your heart centre. It is fascinating to experience how the body responds to these practices.

Poetry as Prayer

I learnt the following practice from talks by Padraig O Tuama, who is a leader of the Corrymeela Community, Northern Ireland's longest established peace and reconciliation organisation. He is a poet, theologian, and mediator, and has worked in conflict resolution in Ireland, Africa, and the Middle East.

He describes the 'Collect', which is an ancient form of prayer that follows five distinct steps to create a poetic form. Within this structure, we can find a way to return to a sense of hope that our deepest aspirations can come into being. It allows us to let go of the egocentric belief that we need to do everything ourselves. We do not need to take on a sense of responsibility for everything, we can ask for help.

Here is Padraig O Tuama's example of the 'Collect':

God of watching,
whose gaze I doubt and rally against both,
but in which I nonetheless take refuge, despite my limited vision.
Shelter me today,
against the flitting nature of my own focus
and bring me to the calm place in which to stand.
And when I falter, which is likely,
give me both the courage and the kindness
to begin again with hope and coping.
For you are the one whose watchfulness is steady.
Amen.

Contemplative Practice: Creative Writing

Look at O Tuama's piece to identify the five distinct parts. Now see if you can use these same sections to create your own prayer:

1. Address your spiritual being or higher power in a fitting way.
2. List their qualities.
3. Make your request.
4. Refer back to the qualities that you believe will help bring the request into being.
5. Offer thanks or a closing phrase.

Here is my own poetic prayer, written with the image of Green Tara in mind. It ends with the mantra that is associated with her:

Beloved Wisdom Moon,
Whose love for all beings was so strong that you stayed with us
in the form of Green Tara.
You are swift, yet still; fierce, yet compassionate,
You know when to take action and when to let others help themselves.
Please help me to rest in silence and know when and how to act
with compassion and wisdom.
I open myself to your unlimited capacity for service to the world
and I invite you to guide me.
I trust in you because you have shown that all is possible.
Om tare tutare ture soha.

Types of Bodhisattva

Buddhist teachings mention three different types of bodhisattva: the monarch, the ferry driver, and the shepherd. Depending on your personality, you may feel more connected with one of these.

Monarchs tend to develop their own strength and confidence, often through studying and deep practice, before they feel ready to help others. It can take them many years to wear their bodhisattva crown, but once they do, they lead with wisdom.

The ferry driver travels on the same ferry as everyone else, in the same direction, but has the responsibility of guiding the way. They learn and teach, teach and learn, along with their community. Everyone is welcome on the journey and appreciates the sense of exploring together.

Shepherds put the welfare of all others ahead of their own, in the same way that they would look after their flock. They are willing to stay outside in the hot sun, rain, or snow, to attend to those in their care.

Which type of bodhisattva best describes your personality? How do you relate to the people around you? Are there inspirational people you know, or know of, who seem to represent one of these categories?

> ### Engagement Practice: Inspirational Changemakers
>
> This practice is designed to put you in touch with the part of yourself that is willing to engage with the outside world. It involves acknowledging your aspirations. It is important to recognise your unique gifts and potential to be of service to others, alongside the work on your shadow aspects. For this reason, you can begin by exploring the qualities of the changemakers that you admire. The person who inspires you could be living, or deceased, or even a mythical being that you aspire to be like.
>
> Bring to mind three or four compassionate activists or changemakers that you admire. They may be people you know personally, or those in the media, or history, who seem to have vast minds.
>
> Note down a) their good qualities, and b) the areas of their life that were most important to them, or what they are/were passionate about.
>
> How do/did they manage to achieve their aspirations?
>
> Now compare your lists and notice any recurring themes or qualities.

> In coaching, there is a saying, "If you spot it, you've got it". Write down your own list of changemaker qualities, starting with "I am..." or "I have..."
>
> Start to own that you have this same potential within you, even if these qualities need a little watering. These might be your Golden Shadow, waiting to be integrated and offered to the people around you. Acknowledge that it might be uncomfortable writing down, and owning, your good qualities. However, once you can own them, you can then use them in service of others.

The Bodhisattva Vow

*"A bodhisattva is someone who has compassion
within himself or herself
and who is able to make another person smile or
help someone suffer less.
Every one of us is capable of this."*
~ *Thich Nhat Hanh*

In many spiritual traditions, people take vows to stay committed; a compass to guide them along the path. The Bodhisattva vow is huge, "Beings are numberless, I vow to free them all." In 2021, I realised I would never be up to the task, so decided to do it anyway, under the gentle and joyful guidance of Yongey Mingyur Rinpoche.

True to form in South Africa, this serious spiritual ceremony became a classic comedy moment. I was co-facilitating a yoga retreat and had arranged the schedule so that I could take the vow quietly, between sessions. I imagined sitting in serene meditation, with my husband at my side, supported by the great Maluti mountain range, while making this serious wish to put the needs of others before my own.

Just before the online ceremony was due to start, Eskom (South Africa's power supplier) pulled the plug out. The wifi in our farmhouse stopped working and the cellphone signal wasn't strong enough. My friend jumped to the rescue, letting me know that there was a generator at the main lodge. She rang ahead to ask for it to be switched on. I packed up the laptop and we hot-footed it to reception, where the generator was already purring. "Where can we get Wifi?" I enquired. "Over there, in the bar. I'll just reboot the router."

And this is where we found ourselves, my husband and I, on bar stools, with one earphone each, our palms together, chanting Tibetan phrases... in the dark corner of a pub! The teachings were so clear and simple that it felt possible. We were vowing not to create more chaos and misery in the world, but rather to work on ourselves while working with others.

Looking back, it feels so fitting. The vow is about navigating daily life, where nothing is sanitised and perfect. It calls for adaptability, and the giving and receiving of support in community. And most of all, keeping a sense of humour, knowing that we are all flawed, yet there is potential for transformation and healing in the midst of chaos. We cannot remove all the thorns from the world we are in, so we may as well put shoes on and train our minds (and feet) to dance lightly through the dirt. As bodhisattvas-in-training, we can be realistic, while still holding onto the potential for vast aspirations.

When Joanna Macy, an environmentalist activist, author, and scholar of Buddhism, was leading a training on The Work that Reconnects, she found herself talking to a monk who asked her about vows. This is quite a common practice within monastic traditions, but not something that we often do in daily life. She recounts how a set of Five Vows of Active Hope came to her in that moment and she offered them to the group. They set a powerful direction and commitment for the group going forward in their work for climate justice:

I vow to myself and each of you:
1. To commit myself daily to the healing of our world and the welfare of all beings.
2. To live on Earth more lightly and less violently in the food, products, and energy I consume.
3. To draw strength and guidance from the living Earth, the ancestors, the future beings, and my brothers and sisters of all species.
4. To support each other in our work for the world and to ask for help when I feel the need.
5. To pursue a daily practice that clarifies my mind, strengthens my heart, and supports me in observing these vows.

> ### Engagement Practice: Vows
>
> Without thinking too much, write down ten aspirational commitments that come to mind. This is just a writing exercise, so let your ideas flow. It can help to recall your good qualities, or connect with your sense of purpose, and turn these into ongoing commitments.
>
> I find it fun to explore the meaning of my name and use that as a guide. In Latin, Lucy is lux, meaning light.
>
> - May I remain light-hearted and share this joy with others.
> - May I be a light to guide all beings during times of darkness.
> - May I support others to find their own guiding light.
>
> Here are some more examples:
> - May I smile at everyone I meet.
> - May I be a sheltering tree, forever growing, yet also willing to provide shade and support to others.
> - May I be a boat to ferry people across difficult waters.
> - May I be a shepherd, caring for all beings.
>
> These ten aspirational commitments can begin to set the compass of your heart through intention. Remember that small daily actions add up to a life of purpose and meaning. Once you feel into them, you can turn these into your own equivalent of a bodhisattva vow.
>
> Now, as your engagement practice, see if you can keep one vow for a whole day.

HOME PRACTICES

1. How is your daily meditation practice going? Do you find a preference for the calming or insight practices, or do you prefer to cultivate your positive qualities? Note the moments of insight and the moments of challenge. They all guide you towards greater self-awareness.

2. Which activities in the chapter did you do this week and which ones did you choose to skip over? Some people love the creative arts

practices and others shy away with the declaration that, "I am not creative." However, we are all creative and this declaration of 'I' is a technique to prevent ourselves from uncovering hidden talents. With this little nudge, see if you can go back and write a poem or a set of vows.

3. Get to know your own compassionate activist by drawing on the inspirational changemaker you identified. Notice the qualities you would like to cultivate and choose someone who best represents your idea of a compassionate activist. Perhaps it is a religious figure like Jesus Christ or the Virgin Mary, or a deity like Chenrezig or Green Tara, or a wisdom keeper such as Vusamazulu Credo Mutwa, or an inspirational ancestor.
- Think about their qualities and how you wish to water those same qualities within yourself.
- Either write a poem, a piece of prose, paint a picture, or make a model from clay, of this image.
- Connect deeply with this image, so that it springs to mind at a time when you most need to access those qualities in yourself.
- Remember that one of the qualities of this being is their ability to turn difficulty into insight, shadow into light, mud into the lotus flower.

When you have decided on your own archetype of the compassionate activist, you can get started. All you need is a commitment to be of service to others in the smallest of ways.

CHAPTER 7
Enlightened Self-Interest

"Bodhisattvas are referred to as enlightened 'heroes' or 'warriors'. They are highly altruistic beings who have the wisdom to realise that by dedicating themselves to the welfare of other sentient beings, the fulfilment of their own self-interest comes automatically as a by-product."
~ His Holiness the Dalai Lama

The Four Limitless Qualities

The first meditation retreat I ever attended was on the Four Immeasurables, where we learnt to recognise, and cultivate, our limitless capacities for goodness. It eased me through a time of deep sorrow as my father had just passed away, and it left behind a velvety coating of serenity, as well as the wish to share the practices with others.

The immeasurable qualities are taught in many Eastern wisdom traditions as essential traits of the spiritual warrior. As relational qualities, they are foundational to the African philosophy of ubuntu, which centres interconnectedness. They are also receiving a great deal of interest from Western psychologists and are known as pro-social qualities that bind families and communities together. We could describe them as the universal qualities that open the door to our altruistic potential, and you may recognise them as part of your own spiritual or religious belief system.

Love, or loving kindness, means wanting everyone, including ourselves, to be happy, and we develop this through a sense of friendliness. Compassion is the recognition that everyone suffers at times, and we wish to alleviate that suffering through a caring presence, kind words, and helpful actions. Empathetic joy involves rejoicing in the good fortune or talents of another, and appreciating our own attributes, too. Equanimity, which reveals itself through a tranquil state of mind, enables us to stay steady when we face hardship, and allows us to see beneath superficial classifications of 'right and wrong', even when others are behaving in ways that we perceive as harmful.

The Four Immeasurables			
Quality	**Definition**	**Practice**	**Sign of Fruition**
Loving-Kindness	Wanting others to be happy	Friendliness towards everyone you meet	Full heartedness
Compassion	Wanting others to be free from suffering	Compassion towards those in distress	Tenderness
Empathetic Joy	Rejoicing in the good fortune of others	Joy towards those who are virtuous or fortunate	Radiance
Equanimity	Regarding all others as equal to oneself	Equanimity towards those who are not virtuous	Ease

These are innate capacities of human beings, and they can be developed further with a clear intention and specific meditation practices. Cultivating these four pro-social qualities has an interesting impact – our own happiness arises as a by-product. What we offer outwards, comes back to replenish us. Equally, by wishing that others experience these states, we increase the likelihood of noticing them within ourselves, and we then have more to give. This is why they are called immeasurable or limitless.

As with all our contemplative practices, we can proceed slowly. The cultivation must not feel forced. We're not pretending anything or making false affirmations. Pema Chödrön, a beloved Buddhist teacher, author, nun and mother, writes about imagining a little spring, that trickles through a crack in the rock. With time and patience, the water erodes the rock face, flowing more freely, and gaining momentum as it moves downhill. Once that little trickle reaches the ocean, it is immeasurable in its vastness.

This is how we approach our practice, with a willingness to believe it is possible to cultivate these qualities, but without rushing to get there all at once.

> ### Contemplative Practice: Four Immeasurables
> These positive qualities are traditionally cultivated during your daily mindfulness practice. Start with some deep breaths or the sensation of your body connecting with the surface beneath you. When you feel your mind settling a little, bring to mind someone that you feel close to, and make the wish:
> - May you be happy.
> - May you be free from suffering.
> - May you find joy.
> - May you be at ease.
>
> Repeat these phrases over and over again, imagining that your loved one is receiving your well wishes. You may also like to adapt the phrases to the specific person, such as "May you feel safe; may you recover swiftly".
>
> After a while, allow their image to dissolve away, noticing the felt sense in your own body. Do you feel warm, cool, numb, tingling, expansive, contracted? Allow whatever is present to be acknowledged. It will disappear in its own time.
>
> Then bring yourself to mind at the age you are now, or perhaps a younger version of yourself.
> - May I be happy.
> - May I be free from suffering.

> - May I find joy.
> - May I be at ease.
>
> You may then expand the circle outwards to include your friends, family, colleagues, members of your community, country, continent, and the world. This is what makes the practice immeasurable; we keep expanding our intention wider and wider.

Some people can find it distracting to speak these words silently. If this is the case, you can simply imagine sending your love, compassion, joy, and equanimity to the north, south, east and west. Andrew Harvey offers a version of this practice where you imagine yourself as a brilliant diamond that radiates diamond-white light. Send that light in the four directions, praying, with whatever words you choose, that all sentient beings everywhere be happy, well, and protected.

When I teach this practice on retreat, participants often feel warmth or expansiveness around the heart centre. Notice if you felt any sensation here. If not, that's okay. Tuning into the body's response to meditation can take time. It's interesting to observe that our chemical balance changes within the body during practices that invite a sense of social connection.

Intentions

Cultivating the qualities of the compassionate activist takes time and requires a clear intention. Be careful not to rush or to expect too much of yourself. The thought of changing ourselves through goals or resolutions, brings many of us out in a cold sweat.

Old habit patterns of striving, rush, and judgement can paralyse our ability to let transformation happen at its natural pace. Most resolutions fail anyway, leaving us feeling more despondent than if we had not made them in the first place! It can be useful to understand the conscious and unconscious processes that support, or often block, our path to spiritual growth.

I've found it helpful to categorise intentions into three types: self-interested, mutually beneficial, and altruistic. Not surprisingly, we tend to be focused on self-interested ones initially, and this is an important first step, because if our basic needs are not being met, we feel threatened and defensive, often projecting our fears and anger onto those around us.

It can be helpful to remember that our needs are as equally important as the needs of others – no more and no less. Depending on your upbringing, you may have been taught to put others' needs ahead of your own. And this can be problematic, if you believe that you are inferior to some, or superior to others.

When we deeply believe that we are all equal, then our own interests, and the interests of others, are given the same weight. Once our basic survival needs have been attended to, we can shift to the second category of intentions, which involves balancing our needs with the needs of others. Our intentions can be mutually beneficial. In the business world, this is often called 'win-win'. In terms of our spiritual growth, this is enlightened self-interest!

The third type of intention is based in altruism. It is only possible once our ego-centric perspective has dissolved – and this takes time. When we understand that we are interdependent and that we can only be truly happy when the people around us are happy, our focus can shift towards true altruism. All our thoughts and actions are in the service of others because we do not need to keep feeding our sense of self.

You have probably experienced these moments already, maybe out in nature, or when you were watching children play. Your sense of self dissolves away, and you experience an upwelling of joy simply by tapping into the living world; into the happiness of others. You do not need to be doing anything, except watching, yet somehow the joy of life gets transmitted to you.

Similarly, when we hear that a dear friend has succeeded at something, we experience a sense of appreciation or empathetic joy. Of course, sometimes, it might be tinged with a little bit of jealousy, and that is because we are human, and still in the process of training our mind. It is rare to meet or hear about people who are wholly altruistic, but it is an attitude to which we can aspire. And paradoxically, the wish to be wholly in service of others is what will bring us the greatest joy.

An ancient book called the 'Way of the Bodhisattva', contains a powerful quote:

> *"All the joy the world contains*
> *Has come from wishing happiness for others.*
> *All the misery the world contains*
> *Has come from wanting pleasure for oneself."*
> ~ *Shantideva*

It seems counterintuitive that misery comes from seeking pleasure. However, feeding our self-interest and grasping after short-term pleasures only offer momentary happiness, rather than the long-term joy of seeking happiness for all.

It is interesting to note that particular hormones are produced and have different effects on us. When we experience pleasure, the body gives us a quick shot of dopamine, but the effect soon wears off, leaving us craving more. When we find happiness through engaging with others, it is serotonin that is released, and this gives us a longer lasting feeling of contentment and joy.

Happiness as By-Product

In the autumn of 2015, I found myself in South Africa with no work permit and not much work, and my mind was repeating its "you're not good enough" mantra. I felt sluggish, depressed, and unmotivated, rationalising that there was no point doing much, as the creative seeds I wanted to plant would just lie dormant until spring. I was quite forlorn and self-pitying!

Somehow, I seemed to have forgotten much of what I'd learned through my mindfulness practice. Where was that self-compassion I can feel so in touch with at other times?

I tried to resist my feelings, analyse them, and change them, but when nothing worked, I succumbed to the sofa with my arms and legs waving in the air like a flipped beetle! This habit of mine is strong.

What I've been taught, of course, is to accept whatever arises, both welcome and unwelcome states, and to give feelings time to move through me – on their terms, not mine. Had I waited quietly, I could have unwrapped the great gift that this period of free time – my autumn bardo – was about to offer, without the pain of resistance!

On 25 April, the earth shook – a massive 7.8 magnitude earthquake. It shook not under my own feet, but under those of the people of Nepal.

A friend of mine was there at the time, trapped in the mountains, before finally getting helicoptered out to join his wife and children. Theirs was a story of reunion, but there were many other stories of lives lost, as well as houses, ancient buildings, temples, and monasteries left destroyed. The remote villages became totally isolated as vehicles were unable to access them and some of the world's poorest were left even poorer.

Within hours of the news, the group of volunteers I'd worked with 10 years before when the tsunami devastated Southeast Asia, had reconnected across the globe, from the USA to Thailand and Vietnam, from Finland to Sri Lanka and South Africa. They'd set up a website, a PayPal account, NPO status, and developed a vision based on our experience in Thailand and a deep knowledge of Nepal and the needs of its people.

We were back in action as #WeHelpNepal. We raised money, mainly from individuals who contributed what they could, as well as larger movements, such as Avaaz. And these funds headed directly to the people on the ground: Manjushri's Helpers, the Yellow House Collective, the Health and Development Society of Nepal, the Rokpa Orphanage, and others. These were the community-based organisations who understood the short term needs of their networks, while helping to support their longer term needs as well, once the larger aid organisations inevitably moved on. The tagline of #WeHelpNepal was "supporting locally-led, corruption-free, Nepal Earthquake relief efforts so that your contributions fund need, not greed."

Connecting both with the people who were suffering, and those who were on hand to provide support, shook me clean out of despondency and back into a world where I believed in Buddha nature – the intrinsic good in every human being. I put my free time to work helping field the stream of emails coming in through the website and preparing updates of the work happening on the ground – the same role I'd once played in Thailand. Time and again, I experienced that when I was able to help others, I could create meaning for myself, and joy arose spontaneously, even in the face of sorrow.

> *"True compassion does not come from wanting*
> *to help out those less fortunate than ourselves*
> *but from realising our kinship with all beings."*
> ~ *Pema Chödrön*

Humans are a prosocial species; we are hardwired to help others and have evolved to enjoy the kinds of giving that reinforce our sense of shared humanity. Canadian social psychologist and professor, Elizabeth Dunn, has shown that giving our time, skills or money can increase our sense of well-being and life satisfaction, but only under certain conditions. These are choice, connection, and impact.

If we give out of a sense of moral obligation, the joy is diminished. We must choose to give freely. Secondly, we get the greatest satisfaction when we form a meaningful bond with those we are helping. Social connection is what transforms generosity into happiness and is why helping within your own community is so beneficial. Finally, we need to be able to envision how our help is making a concrete difference in someone's life. Giving to large charities or organisations can feel too distant.

While Dunn's research focuses on happiness for the giver, we need to be very aware of the impact on those who are receiving. Giving our mindful presence can be the most rewarding of all, allowing deep insight into another person's needs. This ensures that we uphold the dignity of the recipient and empower them, without creating dependency.

Engagement Practice: Support an Organisation or a Cause

Consider yourself a bodhisattva-in-training! The first step is to experience how it feels to offer support to a charity or organisation.

Remember to choose one that feels important to you, or where you have a direct personal connection. Make the commitment today to donate your money or your time. If that is not possible, you can simply sit quietly and say a prayer, or make a wish, for those who need the support of that organisation. Alternatively, you may want to sign an online petition or support a cause in some other way.

After you've done this, reflect on how it felt to offer help. Did it feel enough just to give? Or did you yearn for some type of connection? Were you hoping for thanks or a show of appreciation?

Inner and Outer

As I sat on the stoep sewing a button on my shorts, I was reminded of the Zen poem that touched me in the midst of the first wave of the COVID-19 pandemic. It speaks so beautifully of the benefits of time alone, away from our familiar social interactions, and our fixed identity. It also highlights for me the mirror-like relationship between my inner and outer worlds; when I care for one with a clear intention, the other feels cared for as well.

"Master, how can I face isolation?

Clean your house. Deep down! In every corner. Even the ones that you never felt the courage and patience to clean up. Make your home bright and well cared for. Remove dust, spider webs, impurities. Even in the most hidden place. Your home represents yourself: take care of it, too.

Master, but time is long. After taking care of myself and my home, how can I live the isolation?

Fix what can be fixed and remove what you don't need anymore. Dedicate yourself to the patchwork quilt, sew the start of the pants, sew the worn edges of the dresses, restore a piece of furniture, fix everything that is worth repairing. The rest, throw it away. With gratitude. And with the consciousness that your cycle is over. Fixing and removing what's outside of you allows you to correct or remove what's inside.

Master and then what? What can I do all the time by myself?

Sow! Even a small seed in a vase. Take care of a plant, water it every day, talk to it, give it a name, remove the dry leaves and the weeds that can choke it and steal precious life energy. It's a way to take care of your inner seeds, your desires, your intentions, your ideals.

Master what if the void comes to visit me? If the fear of sickness and death comes?

Talk to them. Prepare the table for them, too, reserve a place for each of your fears. Invite them to dinner with you. And ask them why they came so far to your house. What message they want to bring you. What they want to communicate to you.

Master, I don't think I can do that...

Your question is not to isolate the problems, but the fear of facing your internal dragons, the ones you always wanted to get away from. Now you can't run away. Look in their eyes, listen and you'll find out that they put you against the wall. They isolated you so they could talk to you, like the seeds that can only sprout if they are alone."

I used to think of my inner and outer world, and my body and mind, as separate. But my experience has taught me otherwise. They feel like two aspects of the same whole, bridged by intention and consciousness. They may appear as different dimensions, yet more and more I see them woven together – the warp and weft of experience.

As I clean out the basement, I clear away unskilful habits; as I water the herbs, I wish for an abundant harvest in Southern Africa. On days when I feel energetic and community-oriented, I head to our local park to weed out the blackjacks, or plant succulents and ferns. On other days, when I yearn for stillness and solitude, I sit in meditation, weeding out judgements, and planting appreciation.

We can transform the world from the inside out, and transform ourselves from the outside in.

I recall noticing the same relationship between body and mind on a mediation retreat. I'd always found it easier to meditate after yoga, when my body was settled, but on this retreat, there were no movement practices. I was frustrated and assumed my body would seize up completely. Yet when I accepted the situation, I found the opposite to be true. The more my mind relaxed, the old places of physical tension relaxed, too. Having sat in stillness for a few days, I tried some yoga. Lo and behold, my legs went behind my head, which was somewhere they had not visited for a while!

This learning drove it home for me: the body and mind, the inner and outer worlds, are no longer opposites in my understanding. Rather, they serve as different starting points from which to experience a place of integration and wholeness.

These days, I try to keep things simple. I've always preferred being out and about, actively planning and engaging in projects, but I'm learning to work differently. Now I focus on what calls for attention – a button, a wilting plant, a grieving friend, a research proposal. The pandemic gave all of us such a clear teaching about our interconnectedness and I hope to use that lesson wisely. Instead of getting overwhelmed by all the structures and systems I don't seem able to change, or change as quickly as I'd like, I'll remind myself that caring for whatever is in front of me is caring for the whole world.

> **Engagement Practice: Small Act, Big Intention**
>
> As you go about your daily chores today, see if you can do them with a big intention. Water your plants with the aspiration that all of the places experiencing drought might receive rain. As you wash your dishes, imagine washing away your negative habit patterns. And as you close your curtains at night, imagine tucking everyone safely into their bed for a restful night's sleep.

Near and Far Enemies

When we make the effort to cultivate positive human qualities, it's important to remember that they are aspirational practices, and they may take time to develop as traits. Aspirations differ from affirmations in that we do not need to hide how we feel; we rather focus our attention on experiencing the truth of who we already are. Aspirations contain a willingness to open your heart, with a simultaneous understanding that your heart may well be guarded through conditioning and past experiences. Don't be surprised if you meet resistance.

Each of the four immeasurable qualities has a near and far enemy, or a shadow quality. The funny thing I find each time I set out to develop these qualities, and to share them with others on retreats, is that their near or far enemies appear almost immediately, as if to mock me, thumb on nose and tongue out with waggling fingers. And I say it's 'funny' because we have to offer ourselves a big dose of humour to get through our unskillfulness and mean-heartedness sometimes. I continue to realise that this aspirational journey is not a short, straight road, but a long and rock-strewn adventure.

The Near and Far Enemies		
Quality	**Near Enemy**	**Far Enemy**
Loving Kindness	Conditional Love, Attachment	Hatred, Anger, Contempt, Ill Will
Compassion	Pity, Sympathy	Cruelty
Empathetic Joy	Comparison, Insincerity, Hypocrisy, Overexcitement	Envy, Jealousy
Equanimity	Indifference, Apathy	Prejudice, Discrimination, Anxiety, Reactivity, Paranoia

We need to understand why the near and far enemies appear, so that we can move away from guilt, blame, or shame. As we have learnt already, our brains evolved in three distinct stages, over 600 million years! When we feel under threat, our 'reptilian' brainstem is activated, and we become myopically self-centred. We do what it takes to survive and act from the near or far enemy orientation. Once we are free from daily fears and struggles, we can start to cultivate more positive, pro-social emotions, and get to know the four immeasurables more intimately.

We often experience these 'enemies' when we try to cultivate the real thing, as they cleverly disguise themselves. We experience the near enemies at times when our egocentric preferences are still strong, and we don't feel confident enough in our innately good nature. We experience the far enemies when we are in survival mode, or we've been harmed by others. Or it may be that we believe the welfare of others can only be achieved at our expense. This is not true.

When we connect with the reality of interdependence, we discover that our welfare is dependent on the welfare of others. Relationship is at the heart of these practices; they serve to soften our relationship with ourselves and help to deepen our relationships with others.

Sometimes I have dreams of jealousy and hatred, or I feel rage boiling up at someone who is 'wasting my time'. I experience despondency and a heavy apathy when pondering an intransigent community, or I pretend not to see the car guard who is asking for some small change. I find it easy to fall into self-hatred with an internal dialogue that 'I am a horrible person and a fraud'. Yet I am a human, and I don't always have the capacity for care, especially when my own heart is sore.

During these moments of doubt, I take comfort from a process called 'reciprocal inhibition'. This process supposes that the mind is unable to hold more than one thought or attitude at a time, which means that during the process of cultivating love and friendliness, hatred and contempt cannot arise. All we can do is start where we are, and do the best we are able to, in each moment.

> **Shadow Integration Practice: Near and Far Enemies**
>
> Have a look at the table on the previous page and be very honest. Bring to mind a time in the last week or month when one of the near or far enemies came up for you. Without shifting into shame, guilt, or blame, quietly consider what circumstances you were experiencing at the time. Non-judgemental reflection can give you the opportunity to understand yourself a little deeper, without having to justify or rationalise your unskilful behaviour. Only once we relate to ourselves in a kind way can transformation take place.

The Fruits of Practice

When these pro-social qualities start to arise spontaneously, the experience is ineffable. Words cannot do justice to the visceral expansiveness of the heart, the warm underbelly of tenderness, that sense of ease, when we truly feel that all beings are equal and we can soften back from that competitive struggle and striving. We need to practice in order to experience that these qualities are already a part of us all, biding their time under the armour of self-protection, and waiting to be seen, felt, and shared with others.

It becomes possible not only to expand your sense of connection with those you hold most dear, but also with those you may consider unlovable or who may have hurt you. In the moments of opening up around old wounds, we come to trust how these aspirational practices can deeply alter our relationships, with ourselves and those around us.

As you commit to cultivating these qualities and living a life of purpose with the welfare of others at the heart of your work, you may well move through certain stages. This is normal and it shows that your commitment is bearing fruit.

These stages may include:
1. Uncertainty: you may need to enquire into what you love, or a difficult aspect of your life that you have overcome, that now inspires you to support others in the same position.
2. Intention-setting: being clear is essential to focus and stay committed, even when times get challenging.
3. Sticking with it: despite the tough times, and the realisation that you are flawed, you need to stay grounded and connected with your passion and intention. It is not always just about what you love to do; it's about what you feel is important enough to make a sacrifice for.
4. Offering the benefit: begin your work without rushing to achieve results. When good results do start to emerge, make the wish that the happiness you feel will spread out in ever-widening circles. This is sometimes called 'sharing the merit', where we don't hold on to the feeling of good fortune, but instead, let it expand to benefit all beings.

HOME PRACTICE

1. How is your daily meditation practice going? You can do both formal practice, and informal practice, as part of your daily life. For example, when you are driving, or waiting in a queue with other people around you, experiment with sending out well wishes to everyone you see, aspiring that they might be well and free from difficulties. Notice whether this spontaneous practice changes anything within you.

2. Which activities in the chapter did you do this week and which ones did you choose to skip over? Are you getting a sense of where your own blocks might be?

CHAPTER 8
A Life of Purpose

*"A man's true wealth is the good he does
in this world."
~ Muhammad PBUH*

*"Set your heart on doing good.
Do it over and over again and you will be
filled with joy."
~ Buddha*

When we find a concept that repeats itself across all cultures and religions, we're usually touching into a truth of human existence. Life purpose is one such truth. Ancient wisdom traditions and modern psychological research agree that we're happier when living a purposeful life. What's more, our level of well-being tends to increase if our purpose expands to include the welfare of others.

There is a growing body of research about the health benefits of living a life with purpose. Whether or not we are clear about our purpose, the very act of seeking one increases our levels of well-being. The journey of finding purpose appears to be more important than the final destination. While these findings are drawn from present-day research, it is rooted in ancient wisdom and has been explored in all the spiritual texts.

Some Eastern traditions use the Sanskrit term svadharma, which means our own truth. In Southern Africa, the Zulu word, ubizo, is our calling, both to heal and to be of service to others. The Japanese concept, ikigai, is the place where four aspects of our life intersect – what we love, what we're good at, what we're paid to do, and what the world needs. Ken Robinson, the creativity expert, used the term element, meaning that when we are in our element, our talents and our passion intersect. In French, we use the phrase raison d'etre, our reason for being, and in Spanish, it is the razon de ser.

We are born with talents, gifts, and interests for which we can take no personal credit. We may have inherited them from our parents, or their parents, or they may be something that has been passed down through our genes and nurtured through our upbringing.

First, we need to get to know ourselves intimately, and find the road towards self-awareness. Only then, can we shift our focus to ask, "What can I bring of myself to serve others?", as we offer our gifts to the world.

Jack Kornfield talks of a West African belief in 'delivering your cargo'. West Africa has many rivers and waterways, so the metaphor reveals how we need to carry our personal gifts down river to deliver our cargo to others. Robin Wall Kimmerer, a mother, scientist, decorated professor, and enrolled member of the Citizen Potawatomi Nation, writes on the Native American teachings, which centre gratitude and reciprocity. Instead of hiding or ignoring our personal gifts, we must honour them. All of us can give and receive from a grateful heart, not in a transactional way. And by doing so, we fulfil our responsibility to our gifts, and to those with whom we share our lives.

Finding your Life Purpose

At the beginning of each year, I run retreats on New Year Intentions. I escort participants through a weekend of turning inwards, so that they can touch into their source of joy. Over the years, I've noticed that people can find their life purpose in several different ways.

A few – a tiny few – seem clear on their purpose from the very beginning. They know who they are, and what they want to do, and this intention gives them the courage to stay on course, no matter the barriers that may cross their path. Others can have defining moments, which they don't necessarily recognise at the time, but through a process of retrospection, they come to realise just how deeply impacted they were by those moments.

> "Life can only be understood backwards;
> but it must be lived forwards."
> Søren Kierkegaard

Trevor Noah, the comedian, and South African host of the USA's Daily Show, tells a beautiful story of realising the power of comedy. He was with his grandfather, during an anti-apartheid protest, when a white police officer on horseback drew close to them trying to move the crowd along. The atmosphere was tense. Then Trevor's grandfather told a joke and the police officer burst into a fit of laughter. Tears were even rolling down his cheeks! Everyone around them started to laugh as well.

In his young life, Trevor had never seen a policeman laughing with black African people before, and he keenly felt the potential of a joke to diffuse tension. From that moment, he appreciated the power of comedy for transformation.

Most of us must feel our way, listening for clues, or chasing up a few blind alleys before we realise that we were probably following the right route all along. Sometimes, we don't even need to change what we are doing, but rather how we do it, or the perception we have of our contribution.

When I first moved to Johannesburg, I got caught up in the speed of the city. I was teaching yoga, studying for a PhD, and driving from place-to-place. My attention and energy felt scattered as I followed multiple paths of interest. Then I realised that all the paths were tributaries connected to mindfulness. They were each leading into the same river, and a powerful sense of meaning emerged. Sometimes we don't need to change the external circumstances. Rather, we need only to release the internal sense of struggle or striving. If we have an overall life purpose beyond our ego-centric wants, then we can develop a sense that each step forward is imbued with greater meaning. Most spiritual traditions teach that helping others brings happiness to us, as long as we are giving from a place of fullness.

We often trip ourselves up by assuming that if something comes to us naturally, it must be easy for everyone else, and we can overlook or discount our unique contribution. This also means that we can deny ourselves the opportunity to earn an income from something we love to do; something we are good at.

A quote, attributed to Confucius, reads: "Choose a job you love, and you will never have to work a day in your life", and it certainly has much wisdom in it. But it needs to recognise the commitment required to cultivate a talent or a career.

It is not always an easy ride, but if you love what you do, then you will feel more inspired and more fulfilled, and the income you earn, while being important, won't be your only motivation.

Another way by which we sabotage ourselves is by loving our work so much that we don't feel we want to charge for it. This may come from a place of generosity, but more often, it's rooted in a lack of self-worth, where we feel uncomfortable exchanging our skills for a reasonable income.

We discover our purpose through receptivity, rather than action. It is already present wanting to be heard, seen, and felt. This requires three stages:

- Willingness to listen.
- Welcoming the messenger.
- Willingness to act.

Contemplative Practice: Receptivity

Time in meditation is a powerful way to generate the conditions for insights to arise, to be heard, and ultimately, acted upon. Without tapping into our internal guidance, we tend to react to external demands, often from a place of fear and self-protection, rather than from our inner yearning for self-actualisation.

Poetry also seems to be an effective way to link the rational mind with the world of feelings. It is our feelings that usually inspire action.

Find a comfortable way to sit, and then take five or more deep abdominal breaths, until you feel yourself settling down, and becoming more receptive to the world within you, and around you. When you feel ready, read through the following poem by Martha Graham, and see what arises. Stay open. Trust what emerges within your awareness. Feel into any urges that motivate you.

There is a vitality, a life force,
a quickening, that is translated into action
And because there is only one of you in all time
this expression is unique
And if you block it, it will never exist through
any other medium and will be lost...
The world will not have it
It is not your business to determine how good
it is, nor how valuable, nor how it
compares to other expressions
It is your business to keep it yours,
clearly and directly... to keep the channel open
You do not even have to believe in yourself
or your work...
You have to keep open and aware
directly to the urges that motivate you
Keep the channels open!
~ Martha Graham

Now take time to journal about your findings, taking note of whether any small action steps appear that you could even take today. This is how our receptivity guides us into wise and skilful action.

Intention and Motivation

Our life purpose includes both the intention and the motivation. Some people feel stuck when they cannot identify their unique life contribution and consider this a failure of some sort. This is a mistake. In life, we can ultimately choose to pursue any career. It is the way we do it that becomes important. When our actions are infused with a pure intention, we bring wholeness and humanity into the world.

To identify what is deeply important to you, and gauge whether you are living your intentions, you'll require a constant, present moment, witnessing of the body, the heart, and the head. We need to be aware of the moments in which the body contracts and tightens, or opens and feels spacious and energised.

When you think of a project, and feel a gripping sensation in the body, you then need to be in tune with your heart and feelings. Is it excitement or fear (or both together) that makes you feel tense?

On my first mindfulness teacher training retreat, I remember connecting with an image of sitting on top of a high plateau, looking out over a vast horizon. I felt tingling throughout my body, and a combination of fear and elation. I wondered to myself, was this going to be the new direction in which my teaching career would evolve?

A first step in identifying your life purpose is to tune in and remind yourself about what you love doing. Many people find it hard to identify what their passion might be, as they are not used to opening up emotionally. By looking back on the year, or years, gone by, or reflecting on your childhood, you can highlight the moments of your greatest joy, inspiration, or achievement; those times you felt fully alive and engaged, or even lost track of time; the moments when you felt deeply content, happy, or in a state of flow.

As children we were more in touch with our authentic self, than the externally validated social self that tries to fit in with the opinions of others. See if you can find ways to reconnect with this emotion-driven sense of what you enjoy doing. Trust it, and then commit to prioritising weekly activities that allow you to cultivate your passion.

If you notice that your current work does not feature in the process, this is often a sign that you need to change the way you are approaching your work or improve an overall sense of balance in your life. It does not mean you need to change direction completely. It's subtle shifts that can bring alignment. If you have a yoga or movement practice, you may have experienced this. By activating or relaxing a single muscle, you can change and enhance the entire experience.

One day, during the pandemic, I took a taxi. The driver was attentive, careful, and kind. We talked about the challenges of earning a living during lockdown, about her family, and about the chaos and joys of life in South Africa. She was so grateful to be back behind the wheel, albeit behind a mask as well.

By the time I got to where I was going, I felt I had spent time with a friend. She genuinely wished to transport her clients safely, ensuring they arrived at their destination happier than when they started. And that was certainly the experience she gave to me.

This is purpose. It is the invisible, but tangible quality that infuses throughout the work we do. Earning an income is an indisputable need of modern life. The driver still earned the money she needed for her family, but she chose to add something more to the journey. When we do any job with purpose, we can gain a deep sense of satisfaction from the work we do, and this then impacts others.

Many parents, and particularly women, give up their beloved careers to become homemakers. At times, they are filled with grief over what they left behind, and resentment about the childcare, and the never-ending demands of cooking and cleaning. Yet with a conscious shift in perspective, they can acknowledge this loss, and remember that this role is of profound importance, as they create a place of nurturing and safety to raise future-fit children.

Holding space for both is an act of self-compassion. Shifting perspective can take awareness and training, but it makes a huge difference to what can otherwise be viewed as the mundane tasks of daily life.

One of my Buddhist teachers, reassures us that:

> *"Our ordinary lives can become extraordinary*
> *when compassionate intentions guide all that we do."*
> *His Holiness the 17th Karmapa*

Engagement Practice: Sense of Purpose in Life

This practice can be done as a swift way to recognise your sense of purpose and bring it into your consciousness. Once you can articulate your unique sense of purpose, it can better serve you.

- Find a pad of Post-It notes or cut out 12 small square pieces of paper.
- After grounding and centring through the breath, bring to mind your best qualities; the things you like about yourself on your best days or the positive qualities other people have recognised in you. Maybe you are kind, or joyful, or you speak the truth. Write one quality down on each piece of paper, until you have between four and six. Trust your instincts, without thinking too hard. It should take you no more than a minute.
- Next, bring to mind your values, or the areas in your life that are the most important to you. Perhaps this is family, or community; it may be your work in social or climate justice; or your creative or spiritual practice. Allow the ideas to emerge from you, without thinking about it too much. Write each of these down on a piece of paper, until you have between four and six of them.
- Next, see if you can match the two different sets together. Maybe two of your qualities apply to one valued area of your life. Perhaps one good quality can cover two of your values. It doesn't matter. Use your gut instinct to make the connections and see what you discover.

This might be enough for now. You may have a sense of what is important to you, and how you can use your best qualities in the different areas of your life. Notice, too, whether these areas seem to include the well-being of other people.

Now use what you have discovered to write up your own 'Sense of Purpose in Life'. It doesn't need to be a neat final copy; it is a working document that can guide you through the rest of the book. You can review it at the end to see whether it is still salient or can be modified in some way.

Staying Focused

In 2016, I discovered the following poem, at a time when global politics were taking a sharp turn towards self-interest, and away from the needs of the people that leaders claimed to be serving. There seemed to be a rise in the number of narcissists in positions of power, and it felt to me that the global economy was a form of cannibalistic capitalism, putting our collective future at risk. In addition, Leonard Cohen and David Bowie had recently died, and I was finding it hard to accept the loss of such great artists, each of whom had the power of social commentary.

"This is your assignment,
Feel all the things, feel the hard things, the inexplicable things,
the things that make you disavow humanity's capacity for redemption.
Feel all the maddening paradoxes, feel overwhelmed, crazy, feel uncertain,
feel angry, feel afraid, feel powerless, feel frozen, and then
FOCUS
Pick up your pen, pick up your paintbrush, pick up your damn chin.
Put your two calloused hands on the turntables, in the clay, on the strings,
Get behind the camera, look for that pinprick of light.
Look for the truth (yes, it is a thing, it still exists)
Focus on that light, enlarge it,
Reveal the fierce urgency of now.
Reveal how shattered we are, how capable of being repaired,
But don't lament the break.
Nothing new would be built if things were never broken.
A wise man once said: 'There's a crack in everything, that's how the light gets in"
Get after that light.
This is your assignment."
~ Wendy McNaughton and Courtney Martin

The words of this poem really helped pull me out of the quagmire of meeting hatred with hatred. They brought me back to my own unique place and purpose in the world. I touched into the reciprocal need to support, and be supported by, the people around me.

The Compassionate Activist

This was a good reminder that humans are as capable of profound love and compassion as they are of greed and hatred. We all have the capacity to meet a thousand acts of hatred with a million acts of love.

The poem motivated me to write this book and run courses where changemakers could come together and support each other's work – both inner work and work in the world. I realised how much of our ability to persevere is determined by where we focus our attention. There is so much more that unites us, than divides us, if we are willing to look beyond the world of binaries. And when we can touch into our multidimensional selves, we can give that same respect to others.

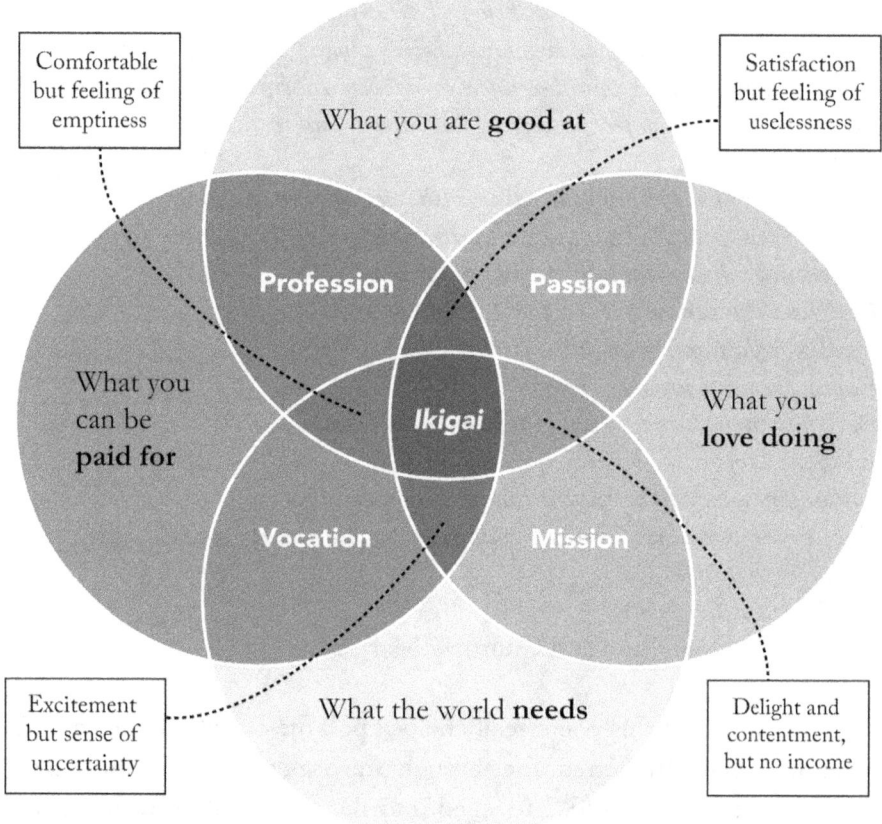

Fig 9 Ikigai

Ikigai

In Japanese, the term Ikigai, means the reason for being, and it is said to be the key to a long and happy life. It is illustrated in Figure 9 above. Your purpose is the central point located between the four areas of activity.

> ### Shadow Integration Practice: Ikigai
>
> The first part of this task is designed to help you identify your Golden Shadow, while the second part invites you to integrate the Dark Shadow that keeps you from living a well-balanced life of purpose.
>
> **1.   Golden Shadow**
>
> First contemplate what you are paid to do, or what you could be paid to do. What are the skills and talents you have that you can exchange with others to fulfil your basic needs? People tend to focus on the extremes. They either focus solely on financial prosperity, or they go to the other extreme of forgetting about the material world, running the risk of becoming a financial problem for other people.
>
> Next look at what you are good at, or what others say you are good at. We sometimes overlook the skills that come naturally to us. It's so easy for us that we tend to dismiss it, but others can more easily see and admire our skills and talents.
>
> What do you love to do? What brings you energy, joy, happiness, and a sense of wonder?
>
> What does the world need, that you can do? If you are a parent, bringing up integrated and kind children, you are doing incredibly powerful work, and the world needs that. Just imagine if all the children at school could talk to each other kindly and hear each other without judgement. Or maybe you're an entrepreneur, growing a business in your hometown, and helping people develop new skills.
>
> Finally, see whether you can identify the unifying aspect. This is something that brings together your profession, your passion, your vocation, and your mission.
>
> Draw your own Ikigai diagram and display it somewhere to remind you.

> **2. Dark Shadow**
>
> Notice which of the circles you feel least able to access. Is it hard for you to tune in emotionally to find out what you love? Is it difficult for you to think beyond your own world, to what the wider world needs from you? Do you find it hard to agree a fair exchange for the talents you have to offer? Do you find it difficult to identify what you are good at? Maybe you even compare yourself with others and discount your own skillsets.
>
> Look again at the diagram and notice whether your tendency is to fall between two of the circles. Does the description in the triangles adjacent to the Ikigai explain how you often feel? For example, if you can connect with your passion and mission, but not the other two circles, maybe you feel delight and a sense of fulfilment, but you struggle with paying the bills.

HOME PRACTICES

1. How are your contemplative practices going? Do you find lots of reasons why you cannot sit quietly for 10 minutes? Or does it now feel like a refuge for you? Are there days when your practice feels supportive, and others when you feel restless? Can you notice the underlying causes?

2. Which other practices in this chapter did you do this week and which ones did you choose to skip over? We can learn so much about ourselves when we notice our priorities and our preferences. This is not a question of 'right and wrong', it is simply a means through which we can gain more information about ourselves.

3. Have you started to get a sense of which side you habitually lean towards: the contemplation or the action? How does it feel to imagine that you could hold both qualities, as a compassionate activist?

CHAPTER 9

Resourcing and Self-Care

*"When you cultivate love and
compassion for all beings,
that means every being, including yourself."
~ Chamtrul Rinpoche*

We all know that life can be difficult; it's just the way it is. And for anyone wishing to change systems, it can be particularly challenging, as we never know whether we'll experience the fruits of our work. How do we get through challenging times, and inhumane and unsustainable systems? Self-care and resourcing are strongly recommended by doctors and therapists who work to support those with the tendency to burn out.

Altruists consistently put the needs of others ahead of their own. However, care and compassion include everyone, even ourselves. We are all equally human – not better or worse. Self-care means choosing to honour our own needs, while attending to the needs of others. One does not exclude the other. We are allowed to look after our painful experiences and human frailties with compassion.

Resources are the activities that help us meet our own needs; they fill us up. They are the tools we can use when times are tough. The more resources we identify, the better. They are as varied as we are. Some people may feel resourced when they go for a long hike, while others may like to sit quietly under a tree. Some like silence; others like music. Some like to paint; others love to dance. Our resources can be effectively matched to our needs.

We need to practice using our resources when things are going smoothly, so that we are in the habit of doing them when we feel depleted. If you are feeling anxious, how do you calm down? If you are feeling despondent and depressed, how can you re-engage?

> **Contemplative Practice: Identifying Your Resources**
>
> Sit quietly, taking some deepening breaths, or simply feeling your connection with the earth. You may also prefer to listen to the sounds around you or notice the shifting sensations in your body. Give yourself permission to settle into a state of witnessing. Bring to mind experiences in the last year when you felt relaxed, or happy, or in a state of flow. What were you doing in those moments?
>
> See if you can name ten resources that you drew on to energise and/or relax yourself? Write them down.
>
> Now reflect on the needs that you often identify in your daily life, and your work, such as needs for connection, peace, vitality, or creativity. You can look at the list at the back of this book to remind yourself about universal human needs (Appendix B). Write down five to ten needs that feel most relevant.
>
> Now see if you can match the tools you use for resourcing with your needs.

A 1000-Year Vision

> *"The world needs to focus both on improving the plight of the world's poor in the short-term and protecting everyone's well-being over the long-term."*
> ~ Tonn

I spent ten years as chair of the Tara Rokpa Centre in South Africa. The founder, Akong Tulku Rinpoche talked to us about a 1000-year vision for the area. When I first heard it, I couldn't make sense of the idea. How could I even begin to imagine what the place would be like in 1000 years, so long after my life span?

With time, however, I realised his wisdom. He was inviting us to move slowly and steadily, not to get bogged down by temporary setbacks. He invited us to be infused with his same vast vision and the sense of expansive potential. We didn't need to do everything immediately. Transformation is a process, and it can be carried out with spaciousness and ease. Everything is possible if we have 1000 years.

We are in this building process together and each of us play different roles. Perhaps you are laying the foundation, or the bricks, or the windows, or the roof, of this metaphorical house. Of course, you want to make every day count, but does that put too much pressure on you? Can you still work steadily and in a way that is sustaining? We need to build foundations that will last.

When I recognised that I would not be around to see the fruits of my labour, I could see that my role is to hand over. Like being in a relay race, my job is to pass the baton to the next generation. In this way, I could learn to work beyond my own ego-centric desires.

Every link in the chain is important and each link supports the whole. This is a shared journey where we do what we can, knowing that not everything will be achieved. We want to begin with the end in mind, so that we infuse our work with a vast intention, yet we also need to remain agile as changing needs arise. Obstacles in our path often open us up to new opportunities and possibilities.

During lockdown, I read the work of Robin Wall Kimmerer, Braiding Sweetgrass. She writes from the Native American wisdom traditions and talks of the Seventh Generation Principle where any decision made must take into account those who come after.

This principle invites us to return our focus to the well-being of the collective. The indigenous worldview is based on reciprocity between humans and the environment – we need each other. This is not how current political planning works, with its 5-year targets, but it is what is necessary now to ensure the survival of humanity on this planet.

Both the 1000-year vision, and the 7th Generation Principle, demand us to see our individual selves in relationship with our ancestors and descendants. When we are asked to make decisions, we do so by considering the long-term outcomes, not just the immediate benefits. This requires responsibility, yet it also takes the weight off our weary shoulders. We are encouraged not to take ourselves too seriously; to play our role as best we can, in our lifespan, while recognising that we do not need to take all the burden, or indeed any of the credit. We can shift from the praise and blame tug-o-war to a place of interconnectedness and reciprocity.

Of course, you only truly have the present moment. The past is memory, and the future is imagination. So, you can focus on what is meaningful to do right now. Small daily activities, carried out with a big intention, can nudge us in the direction of hope.

> ### Contemplative Practice: Your 1000-Year Vision
>
> Once again, relax into a reflective state, whether you are sitting or lying down. Wait a while until you feel your heart rate and breath slowing down naturally. You may find that you sigh or yawn - this is a sign of shifting into a state of inner balance.
>
> Imagine how the world could be in 1000 years, if your vision and all of your hopes come true? Take some time to let these images or the felt sense of this ideal world emerge before you move on to the next reflections.
>
> Now ask yourself, what do I see by the end of my own lifespan, when I pass on the baton to the next generation of vision holders?
> - What will I do next week to move in this direction?
> - What could I do today?
> - What can I do right in this moment?

Living the Future

There is a saying amongst activists: 'Live the way you'd like the world to be.' I've found it such a useful way of bringing the future into the present moment. If I want to live in a caring world, then I can show care for members of my family or community. If I want to see the end of hunger, I can grow vegetables or herbs and share my produce with others. If I want people to be motivated by love and compassion, then it is important for me to be compassionate to myself, even when I do not meet my own aspirations.

On my annual New Year Intentions retreat, I invite participants to connect with an image that represents their aspirations for themselves. The metaphor contains within it all their best qualities in symbolic form. One year, the image that came to me was a huge sheltering tree with roots deeply connected to the earth. My wish for myself was to have branches spreading wide, providing shade and support to others. I could even picture some sweet fruits, ripe and ready to offer nourishment.

A few years later, I was delighted to co-facilitate a retreat for HIV positive youth. We listened to them and we gathered their stories of diagnosis, shame, resilience, and advocacy, and published them in a book called 'Young, Gifted and Positive'.

To remind these youth of their own resources and give them confidence, a narrative therapist took them through a Tree of Life process. Connecting with positive aspects of themselves gave them a deep-rooted strength and an ability to reach out into the world. They left the retreat feeling uplifted and connected to their diverse forest of peers.

I'd previously learnt from Gogo Rutendo Ngara, healer and engineer, that in African cosmology, the tree is the closest relative to humans. At the retreat, it became clear to me as I watched these youth, that through the Tree of Life process, they now felt part of a much larger family of living beings.

Fig 10. The Sheltering Tree

Contemplative Practice: The Sheltering Tree

Draw and label your own sheltering tree, considering the follow questions:

- What are your roots? Perhaps they represent your family history, your ancestors, or your culture.
- What is the ground in which your tree is planted? What do you think of as home? What holds you grounded?
- What is contained in your trunk? What gives you strength, structure, and steadiness? What are your qualities, skills, and knowledge?
- What do your branches represent? What are they growing towards? What are your vision, hopes, and dreams, for the future?
- What do your leaves represent? Who are the important people in your life? Look at the leaves that have fallen, too. What leaves have you lost?
- What bugs are living off your tree? What annoys or frustrates you in life?
- What fruits are growing on your tree? What are the gifts and talents that you were born with and can offer to others?

Working with the sheltering tree is a way to illustrate your hidden stories of strength, resilience, and support. It can also remind you of your personal ecosystem. We are all connected to family and community, and we also contain many resources within us. What's more, when we climb the tree, we can see the horizon. We return to a sense of potential. And we can find creative ways to solve the problems we've experienced in life.

Don't be surprised to see that there are bugs in your tree ecosystem. Aspects of our lives will still frustrate us; it's normal. It is the way that we respond to those bugs that determines how we will grow.

To overcome the challenges of a changemaker's life, we need to find ways to resource ourselves, and to tell the stories of our lives in ways that are sustaining. Using metaphor can take us into the creative parts of our brain and give us different ways of looking at something, so that we don't feel so stuck. Metaphor is central to the way we think, find meaning, and make decisions.

Deep Listening

Researchers at the Max Planck Institute in Germany have conducted various social neuroscience studies. One such study shows that meditating with another person, using contemplative dyads (pairs), can promote social connectedness, reduce social stress, and offer protection against loneliness and isolation.

When we practise deep listening, without the need to interrupt, this can increase feelings of closeness and strengthen our relationships with friends, partners, and even our co-workers. In addition, when we are listened to and not judged, it can reduce our fear of being vulnerable with another, opening us to meaningful social connection. These practices help us communicate with more presence of mind and greater empathy, so that we can become more aware of our feelings and needs, and stay open to the feelings and needs of others.

See if you can get the chance to practice contemplative dyads this week. The instructions are the same as in Chapter 4, but this time, you can practice holding the space for experiences of difficulty.

Remember that there is no need to find a solution or to fix the person you are listening to; you need only to listen without judgement to whatever they're willing to share with you. It is not back-and-forth asking. The role of the listener is simply to listen with your whole body, giving the speaker your full attention.

Engagement Practice: Contemplative Dyads

Choose a partner you feel comfortable with, in person, on the phone, or online. Explain the practice before you begin.

Partner A will ask a question, and Partner B will answer it, giving as much detail as they feel comfortable.

When they become quiet, Partner A says, "Thank you," and asks the same question again.

Repeat the question until the timer runs out – three minutes is usually long enough.

Partner A then reflects on what they heard. This can help to deepen the sense of being seen and understood, which is important for relationship building or repairing.

> After a moment of stillness and silence, switch roles.
>
> Questions to experiment with:
> - What difficulties did you experience this week?
> - What worries you most about the future?
>
> After the dyad practice, reflect on the experience with your partner.
> - Note any physical sensations, feelings, or thoughts that arose within you, while you were listening to the other person.
> - Note any physical sensations, feelings, or thoughts that arose within you, while you were speaking to the other person.
> - Describe the relationship between you before and after the practice.
> - How did it feel for you to listen without having to think of an answer? Is this usual for you or does it differ from your normal communication style?

Delight and Wonder

The evolved part of our human brain is able to recognise moments of delight and wonder. As you sit here right now, take note of anything that feels supportive or comfortable. Maybe the warmth of the sun or the community of those around you. Touch in to how this impacts the body. How does the body respond to a sense of safety and support? Soak up any replenishing experiences.

Practices of savouring and celebration help train us to bring our brain into balance, so that we are not always drawn into survival mode or negative thoughts, but we can support ourselves to bring equal focus to what is good.

> ### Contemplative Practice: Savouring
>
> Take a journey back through the last week or month, and recall a time of success or delight. Bring that moment into your heart and mind, remembering who was there and what happened.
>
> Recognise any pleasant sensations and allow yourself to bask in the experience. Bring intimate attention to it. How did it feel in your body at the time? What emotions were you experiencing?
>
> Recognise those feelings and allow them to return to you now, so that you can experience them fully. Bring to mind any supportive thoughts you had, such as 'I did it', 'It's finally happened', or similar. Note the voice tone, and recognise those self-supporting words or the words of others. Allow yourself to bask, and soak it in, savouring the wholesome and inspiring moments, so that you learn to feel them more deeply.
>
> Notice where your mind is and invite it back to the present moment if it has wandered. Feel the points of contact with the earth, the gentle flow of the breath, the community that is supporting you. Savour what is good and imagine transmitting it out to all beings. Visualise how the world would be if everyone could touch into their own moments of delight or joy, happiness, or connection. Make the deep wish that we may all be happy and free from difficulties or else, capable of using those difficulties as the compost in which to grow something beautiful.

Moments of Celebration

When we work in intransigent fields of social or climate justice with a long-term vision, it is hard to see any progress. However, if we make the commitment to keep marking moments of success or recognition, then it gives us the momentum to keep moving forward. The backward gaze allows for forward momentum.

Writer, historian, and activist, Rebecca Solnit uses the metaphor of rowing backwards guided by a coxswain. We may not be able to see where we are going, so we have to trust in a vision, or what emerges in the moment, and adapt our direction or work based on what arises.

She tells the story of a small group of women activists, standing outside the White House in the pouring rain, protesting against nuclear weapons. They felt foolish at the time, assuming their campaign was futile. Years later, though, one of those women heard a high profile activist saying that he had taken the issue seriously when he had seen how passionately committed they were. The women had no idea that their tiny protest would have such an impact, but it was hope that guided their actions. We never know when we will impact someone, but we do know that eliciting empathy is one of the best ways to do so.

> *"Emotion can serve as a powerful motivator, propelling individuals towards certain action tendencies."*
> ~ *Jocelyn Sze & Margaret Kemeny*

When we feel connected to an issue, we act on it. We store information that has touched us emotionally. We need to resource ourselves by gazing backwards and celebrating as often as possible, marking moments consciously so that we are resourced by times of delight. This process provides the momentum for getting through times of despondency.

When we've experienced times of real difficulty, simply attending to daily life tasks can serve as moments to celebrate. Getting through one day in which we do no harm is a real success!

Thich Nhat Hanh talks of the 'joy of the non-toothache'. We're so aware of the pleasant and unpleasant, but we forget the neutral. Once we have experienced deep pain, the neutral moments become ones that can sustain us, too.

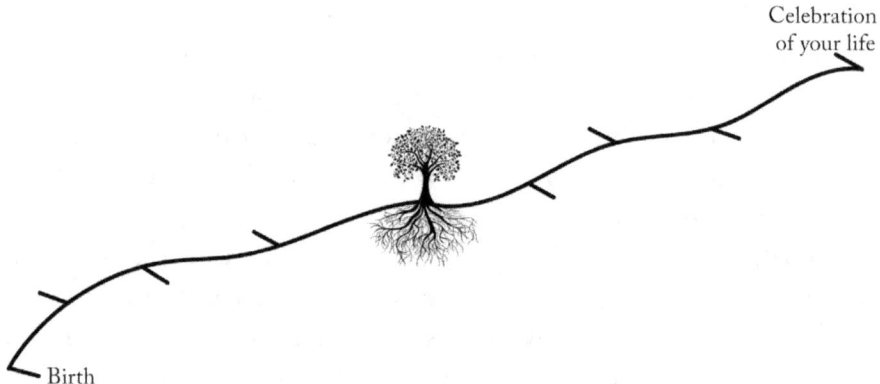

Fig 11. Celebration Timeline

> **Engagement Practice: Your Celebration Timeline**
>
> Draw your own timeline, similar to Figure 11, honouring the moments in your past when you had reason to celebrate.
>
> Notice the ways this activity impacts on your vision for your own future. Can you imagine moments of celebration in the months and years ahead?

Sustainable and Sustaining

"Have you noticed that when we die, our eulogies celebrate our lives very differently from the way society defines success?"
~ Arianna Huffington

We can monitor our own success in terms of how much joy we find in our work, and how much energy we have to keep going, even in the face of complexity and overwhelm. The quiet activist, the role model of peace and wisdom, is extremely powerful. When groups of quiet compassionate activists come together, they make up a force that can withstand all challenges. Our work needs to be not only sustainable, but also sustaining.

Work that Sustains	
Sustainable	**Sustaining**
Big vision - shared by all	Vast vision - beyond our own life span
Rejection of dualistic thinking or othering	Recognition of interconnectedness and interdependence
Compassionate self-reflection and awareness of intention	Clarity of intention - reflection on the 'why' of what we do
Sustainability steeped in self-care	Deep awareness of relationship
Patience to keep moving forward	Celebration of moments of success

> ### Contemplative Practice: Measuring Success
>
> What we perceive as success, and what others recognise as success, may be different.
> - Write down how you measure success, for yourself and others.
> - Which community gives you validation?
> - Whose opinion is important to you?
> - What are the moments that allow you to exhale?

HOME PRACTICES

1. Bring to mind the resourcing practices you identified that are carried out in community, such as coffee with a friend or attending a yoga class. Make sure you do one of those practices this week, and be conscious of how you feel when your community is there to support you.

2. Did you make time to set up a Contemplative Dyad this week? If not, can you get a sense of where your resistance lies? If you did, was there a subsequent effect in terms of the way you listened to other people in your life?

3. Look back through the Foundational Practices at the start of this book.
   - Which ones have been easy for you to complete?
   - Which ones are you still doing on a daily or weekly basis?
   - Where did you notice blocks with the practices?
   - If you noticed that some of these practices are both inward and outward (i.e. the forgiveness of other requires forgiveness of self), how did it feel to do them?
   - Now choose one that you have been resisting or find difficult and commit to doing it this week. Which will it be and why?

CHAPTER 10

Joy as Insurrection

"Joy doesn't betray but sustains activism. And when you face a politics that aspires to make you fearful, alienated, and isolated, joy is a fine act of insurrection."
~ *Rebecca Solnit*

Selflessness and Joyfulness

It's worth repeating... Whether we study psychology, contemplative neuroscience, or Buddhist philosophy, or connect with theistic religions such as Christianity or Islam, the message is the same: we become more joyful when we are in the service of others.

Psychological research around sense of purpose reveals that we have a longer life expectancy if our purpose includes the well-being of others; while neuroscience shows that the parts of our brain associated with well-being light up when we think about helping others. The bodhisattva-in-training feels gladness in witnessing the happiness of others. When we put our personal wants aside to offer help, the by-product is that we become happier. It's counter-intuitive; we think we need to look after our own desires to be happy, yet helping others serves us better.

But what about all of us who become overwhelmed and burnt out while being of service? Where is the joy then? What are we missing?

The Value of Empathy

Empathy is the ability to share the feelings of others. Certain professions require empathy, such as therapists, social workers, or medical doctors, and their professional curriculum even offers empathy training. The recognition that someone is suffering is a prerequisite for taking action. We need to feel to fully respond.

Research has also shown that patients' health can improve more quickly if they experience their caregiver as empathic. When people feel that they are understood and genuinely cared for, they seem able to heal more effectively. However, there can be significant negative consequences for the professional, who ends up experiencing repetitive distress.

Empathy training increases our tendency to react to normal everyday situations with negative emotions because our sensitisation to suffering is increased. Worryingly, research has shown that feeling another person's difficult feelings is a highly aversive experience, and therefore, it can put us at risk of burnout, even though it is beneficial for the client or patient.

Whether we experience pain, or witness pain in others, there is neuronal activation in the same parts of the brain – the anteria insula (AI) and the anterior medial cingulate cortex (aMCC). This mirroring process is called empathic resonance and it means that we pick up other peoples' emotions and feel them. We suffer when we experience the suffering of others and connect with their pain through empathy.

We may have the wish to help, but if we experience vicarious trauma or secondary suffering, it is not sustainable and certainly not sustaining. Our work then drains and depletes us, rather than nourishing and enlivening us.

So, what can be done?

The Missing Link

While conducting empathy research with Matthieu Ricard, a Buddhist monk and experienced meditator, the brain scanning team noticed an unusual outcome. They expected his anteria insula (AI) and anterior medial cingulate cortex (aMCC) to light up as it had with the other research participants, but something completely different happened. Although he was asked to look at photos of terrible tragedy, the neuronal activation occurred in unexpected parts of his brain – the medial orbitofrontal cortex and others – which are associated with feelings of well-being, positive affect, love, and affiliation.

On being asked about what had happened in the scanner, Ricard explained that his Buddhist training is to activate compassion in the face of suffering and in response to the negative feelings triggered by empathy. While viewing the disturbing photos, he had felt natural and boundless love for those suffering and he'd experienced the wish to approach and console them. It was compassion that had strengthened his positive emotions. You may have heard the expression 'compassion fatigue', but it's incorrect. Ricard describes it more accurately as 'empathy fatigue'.

The contemplative neuroscience field has provided us with some remarkable findings that validate what meditators have long experienced. Compassion training is the way to increase our inner resilience and support us in finding joy amidst difficult and emotionally triggering work. Our wish to alleviate others from their suffering makes us happy.

Compassion is generally categorised as a motivation, rather than an emotion, yet it is enhanced or limited by certain emotional states. We're able to cultivate a compassionate motivation most effectively when we are in balance. Fight, flight and freeze emotions reduce our ability to experience compassion. If we are self-absorbed, we cannot perceive the needs of others and if we are feeling strong emotions like anger, disgust, or jealousy, we can't experience compassion. Similarly, we cannot feel compassion if we have too little emotion, or feel disconnected, numb, or overwhelmed.

Compassion can best be cultivated if we are aware of others and emotionally regulated. Interestingly, increasing the motivation to support others down-regulates our sympathetic nervous system (the fight and flight mode), increasing the likelihood of feeling kind. It may seem counterintuitive, but we've all experienced it, and science has provided an explanation. When we shift attention away from our own ego-centric desires, and connect with meeting the needs of others, our innate joy arises.

Compassion as Resilience

Empathy and compassion are distinct inner states with very different consequences for subjective well-being and health. Engagement is called forth in us in the face of sorrow and fortunately, the very act of supporting others can develop remarkable capacities of resilience within us. A monk once told me that he had been suffering from depression, until his teacher told him to work at a soup kitchen. Helping others in such a direct way helped him, even at a time when he did not feel he had much to offer.

> *"A compassionate life is full of positive emotions and feelings of social closeness."*
> ~ Bethany Kok

Feeling the painful experiences of others, while wishing to alleviate their suffering invites an outward-moving tendency, a pro-social wish, to act for another's benefit. Compassion is both fierce and gentle. While sometimes dismissed as soft and fluffy, it can also be a surgeon's scalpel, slicing through a suppurating boil to find what is lodged beneath.

While empathy feels aversion when witnessing someone else's wounds, compassion moves towards the wound and looks deep within. It recognises wounds that will heal on their own, and by doing so, boost the immunity of the wounded. It distinguishes between self-healing injuries and wounds that need an intervention.

Compassion might look passive, yet it knows that when we jump in to rescue others, we disempower the one who is experiencing the natural pain of life. It has boundaries, clear and defined: 'This is yours to attend to; this is mine. I will only step across the line when I have skills or insight that you are currently unable to access. Or when I know that you can learn best with a mentor holding your hand.'

Compassion adapts its wisdom to each and every moment, sometimes stepping up and sometimes stepping back. This motivation empowers both the giver and the receiver, bringing mutual benefit. It is relational and resilience building. It does not take power from one to build up another. That is pity, which infiltrates in the face of pride and neediness.

Compassion may feel like a severing sword for the person causing harm, but it protects many others, and ultimately encourages the perpetrator to suffer less by making them look honestly at their own harmful behaviour. We don't harm others unless we have been harmed ourselves. Compassionate action is grounded in an ethic of care, and leaves space for restorative justice and rehabilitation.

Tonglen

There is a meditation practice often taught to those working in palliative care, as it provides direct training in compassion. It is found in Tibetan Buddhism and is known as tonglen, which means giving and receiving, by using the rhythm of the breath. In the place between the inbreath and the outbreath, transformation takes place, and all difficulties are transformed into compassion. When His Holiness the Dalai Lama was asked about his daily practice of tonglen, he replied:

> *"Whether this meditation really helps others or not,*
> *it gives me peace of mind.*
> *Then I can be more effective,*
> *and the benefit is immense."*
> ~ HH the Dalai Lama

Contemplative Practice: Tonglen Meditation

Sit comfortably and consciously relax. Generate an intention for yourself and/or the benefit of others.

We use the breath for receiving and then giving. Imagine, as you inhale, that you are breathing in something dark, heavy, or murky. Allow any difficulties that you inhale to be spontaneously transformed in the heart. It might feel like water dropping into a hot pan which immediately evaporates into steam. On the exhale, imagine breathing out something that is light, bright or spacious. Continue the practice, allowing the body to feel like an ever widening, clear container of freshness. The exhale is the antidote to whatever you are bringing in.

Invite in a personal issue: the inbreath portrays the feeling tone of any difficulty you're currently having (unworthy, unlovable, frustrated, etc). Each inhale welcomes more of this issue. Allow yourself to trust in whatever way you see this issue. With each exhale, visualise yourself growing more open and bright, like a clear sky over the ocean, with more and more space for the issue to be held in. We may visualise blackness and heat on the inbreath, and turquoise and coolness on the outbreath. Notice the ever-widening embrace of the exhale. The inhale is like a loving parent, willing to hold the full experience of a child's turmoil without judgement. We are not fixing the issue or pushing it away; we are creating a holding environment for the issue to be breathed in, and for the outbreath to allow ever more space for it to move through.

We use this technique as a way of bonding with others. Breathe in the issue for everyone who is feeling the same way in this moment. This is no longer your own problem, but a feature of the human predicament. Life touches us in this poignant way. The outbreath swells our inner body to accommodate the imagined pain of our fellow human beings who share this pain. May we all be willing to meet this pain with fresh space and empathic connection. We are supporting ourselves while under duress, as we simultaneously connect with others, and undermine our habits of isolation during vulnerable experiences.

[This version is drawn from the work of Sarah Powers, founder of Insight Yoga, which integrates the eastern wisdom traditions of Hindu yoga and Buddhist meditation with Western psychology.]

Joy as a Practice

Two of the world's most joyful men – His Holiness the Dalai Lama and Archbishop Desmond Tutu - experienced great hardships in their lives. Yet each of them found the strength and courage to be of remarkable service to their communities and offer sanity in a chaotic world. In their publication, 'The Book of Joy', they revealed how joy and sorrow are intimately linked. It is only when we are willing to face sorrow that we can connect to the wellspring of joy.

Joy is a state, but it is also a practice. The word 'joy' originates from the latin gaudere, meaning rejoice. This is a verb – an action word. Like a muscle, it gets stronger through focused attention and regular use. Joy is a state of being that arises in relationship. It seems to emerge through our willingness to connect with something outside of ourselves. We rejoice in another's good fortune; we delight in a moment of awe.

What is your felt sense of joy?

Personally, I experience a sensation like bubbles, rising from within, and it happens at moments of connection, when my mind shifts from a focus on myself to a focus on another, or on an object of beauty.

Joy comes, not from massaging my ego-centric self, but from losing it in the appreciation of another. Joy is a by-product if you like, of sharing, gratitude, generosity, and attention. It sneaks up on you when you're not worrying about yourself or comparing your life with others; when you are present with what is here, without resistance.

> *"He who grasps to himself a joy doth the winged life destroy;*
> *he who kisses the joy as it flies lives in eternity's sunrise."*
> *~ William Blake*

Joy can't be grasped, but it can be cultivated and savoured, becoming a powerfully sustaining force in your work as an activist. When you can cultivate gratitude, patience, love, and hope, while also transforming hatred, greed, ignorance, jealousy, and pride, then you will surely experience joy.

It is always present when we connect with our true 'being' nature. You do not need to be in a constant state of overwhelm and sadness to be a changemaker. Instead, you can sustain yourself by connecting to the joy of being able to use your talents, accomplishments, or education, in the service of others.

Joyful Activism

> *"Peace-making doesn't mean passivity. It is the act of*
> *interrupting injustice without mirroring injustice, the act of*
> *disarming evil without destroying the evildoer, the act of finding*
> *a third way that is neither fight nor flight but the careful,*
> *arduous pursuit of reconciliation and justice.*
> *It is about a revolution of love that is big enough*
> *to set both the oppressed and the oppressors free."*
> *~ Shane Claiborne*

Work as a joyful, compassionate activist will require you to become aware of the harmful aspects of human nature, to empathise, and then to act with a wholehearted motivation. To this end, you will keep having to reflect how to act in a skilful way that won't drain you.

As compassionate activists, the spiral around which we move can be summarised with the acronym ACE:
- Awareness
- Compassion
- Engagement

I have found mindfulness meditation a trustworthy method of enhancing my awareness. The more I practiced, the more emotions I'd feel, and the more thoughts I'd witness. To begin with, I became more aware of the difficult end of the emotional spectrum. It felt like I had no skin; I empathised more with others and become sensitive to everything and everyone. I no longer had my habitual barriers in place, and this caused me a lot of suffering. I wanted to resist the unpleasant experiences. It's a natural instinct. All animals do; we move away from pain or danger, towards pleasure or safety. But when I tried to suppress or block discomfort, I'd use a tremendous amount of energy trying to resist something that was already present. When I noticed the fear of feeling the pain and sorrow of life, I tried to sanitise my feelings.

I wondered whether to just stop engaging. Yet deep down I knew that difficulties are an inevitable part of human life. When we block unpleasant experiences, we run the risk of losing the spontaneous experiences at the other end of the spectrum: wonder, awe, and delight. Cultivating mindful awareness was a great start, but I couldn't stop there. The next step was to cultivate heartfulness. Mindfulness and heartfulness are often described as two wings. The bird cannot fly without them both.

As my heartfulness strengthened, I was better able to tune in to the joys of the present moment. I'd notice the smell of jasmine or the new flowers on the wisteria. Yet I also felt the pain of a friend facing cancer, another grieving the passing of her mother, or the hunger of the homeless. It was hard to acknowledge, but I could only experience joy when I was willing to come face-to-face with my sorrow and pain. We spend so much time suppressing sorrow, hiding from disappointment and frustration, and distracting ourselves from difficulties, that we have no energy left for joy.

By pulling our emotions from the extremes to a socially acceptable middle range, we lose the powerful, transcendent experiences that sustain us through the sorrow and difficulties. We need to find a way to open up to the full spectrum of human experience by understanding what emotions can offer us.

For me, this meant matching my mindfulness with a deeper understanding of the concept of impermanence. I noticed how I would feel more deeply, but the emotions didn't stay for long. When I became acutely aware of impermanence, I could see that things move and change all the time. I realised I had the ability to let emotions pass through, without needing to cling on to them. This has helped me, and I hope it has helped me be of greater service to others. If I notice someone suffering, I can support them in that moment knowing that at a certain point, they will find the strength within themselves to hold the pain, or the pain itself will move through. Understanding impermanence really helps me to be present for another's pain, without feeling depleted or feeling the need to rescue them.

We use the training of the mind to physically change the structures of the brain. If we are constantly supporting our brain to develop its higher capacities, then things become easier for us. When our limbic system gives us emotional information, we can respond to it skilfully, rather than feeling triggered. We feel more, yet suffer less. Then we can engage with skill and heart.

We're all hard-wired to compassion, so we don't need to struggle; we are simply finding our way back to our original state, rather than developing a new skill. However, as we mentioned in Chapter 5, our innate form of compassion is often considered to be restricted to our in-group, and our capacity must be trained to work with out-groups as well.

Oxytocin was originally called the love hormone, but has lately been termed the tribal hormone, because we are protective of the in-group, but can be aggressive to any potential threat or an out-group. We've seen examples of in-groups turning on out-groups and behaving in ways that seem to lack humanity. Awareness and compassion training are designed to develop the sense that every being is part of our in-group. The work is about expanding the reach of compassion to all living beings, whether animal or human.

> ### Engagement Practice: Collective Action
>
> A good place to end this course and start engaging is to look within your own community to take collective action. Many people are suffering right on our doorsteps. See if you can find out who they are and what they need. Then invite six of your friends or colleagues to help meet those needs.
>
> Andrew Harvey talks about activating the heart of your community: "In my experience, more people than you may imagine are longing to be of help; take the first step now yourself and be surprised and heartened."
>
> Often people just need a little encouragement, and they are very willing to offer support. This may start as a once-off intervention to develop your confidence in taking collective action. Remember these individual initiatives can gain momentum and become the start of something larger and more sustainable.

The Interconnection of Joy and Sorrow

Joyful activism requires a transcendence of the momentary experiences of joy and sorrow. Through transcendence it becomes a practice to transform joy from the ephemeral to an enduring trait, or as Douglas Abrams writes, "From a fleeting feeling to a lasting way of being." Joy provides the fuel that resources the work of the compassionate activist.

We act because of our sorrow at the state of the world, because of our experiences of violence and oppression, of racism, sexism, and all types of bias and fear. Yet the willingness to act from a compassionate motivation is what brings joy.

Joy and sorrow coexist; they're inseparable. When we explore this with a rational mind, it feels paradoxical, but when we touch into the experience of the embodied mind, we know this to be possible. The body can experience a sore, restricted shoulder, while the rest of it is able to move. We can be both victim and survivor and contain both the suffering and the hope of transformation, as well as the ability to move through incredibly difficult circumstances. Humans have an indestructible essence that trusts in its own ability to heal.

"Your joy is your sorrow unmasked.
And the self-same well from which your laughter rises was oftentimes filled with your tears.
And how else can it be?
The deeper that sorrow carves into your being, the more joy you can contain.
Is not the cup that holds your wine the very cup that was burned in the potter's oven?
And is not the lute that soothes your spirit, the very wood that was hollowed with knives?
When you are joyous, look deep into your heart and you shall find it is only that which has given you sorrow that is giving you joy.
When you are sorrowful look again in your heart, and you shall see that in truth you are weeping for that which has been your delight.
Some of you say, "Joy is greater than sorrow," and others say, "
Nay, sorrow is the greater."
But I say unto you, they are inseparable.
Together they come, and when one sits alone with you at your board, remember that the other is asleep upon your bed.
Verily you are suspended like scales between your sorrow and your joy.
Only when you are empty are you at a standstill and balanced.
When the treasure-keeper lifts you to weigh his gold and his silver, needs must your joy or your sorrow rise or fall."
~ Kahlil Gibran

This is where we might contrast compassionate activism with other activist orientations. All activism is rooted in the same experience of responding to causes of harm, but compassion helps us to refrain from hatred. Anger is a fire that can be well-contained in its hearth and used to keep us warm and motivated, or it burns wildly, causing damage and destruction all around. Compassion does not burn out; it sustains itself.

This involves a shift from the archetypal masculine to a feminine orientation; from retributive justice to restorative justice that is rooted in an ethic of care. Joyful activism calls on us to face the tragedies and suffering that are part of our current global experience. From this place of truth and clarity, we cultivate compassion and shift focus to intentional action.

We need to connect with moments of hope to give ourselves the vitality and strength to face despair head on. Most of all, though, we must sense our interconnectedness. We connect with others, and move forward in solidarity. Once you feel connected to others, and are living your own meaningful life, then joy is sure to land upon your shoulder.

> ### Engagement Practice: Your Path Ahead
> Ask a friend to play the role of a benefactor who is willing to give you all the money, resources, personnel, technological support, and anything else, you might need to bring your idea to serve others into being.
> - Tell them exactly what you will do given the support you need.
> - Let your ideas flow as you present them to a supportive person who believes that what you want to do is important.
> - Consider recording what you are saying to them and then write the ideas down for future reference.
> - Now decide what you can do today to set you off in this direction, with nothing more than you have right now.

HOME PRACTICES

This week, I suggest you take time to be guided by this Intention Setting Meditation. It has been adapted from a Loving Kindness Meditation by B Alan Wallace and I've used it on retreats to help participants connect with their heart's deepest desires in order to live a life of joy and meaning.

Begin by making yourself comfortable, either in a chair or lying down, or sitting cross-legged on the floor. You may like to do this practice quite often, perhaps every Monday as you begin a new week of life. Allow a regular time of practice to check in with your heart's intentions and aspirations.

Committing and Connecting:

We begin every practice with a commitment, maybe bringing your hands together at the heart and wishing deeply that you can bring mindful awareness to the body, heart, and mind; knowing it is for your own deepest well-being and for the benefit of all those with whom you share your life. Commit to aligning your heart with kindness and compassion, knowing that it will naturally spread out to others. Release your hands to a comfortable position and soften into your body. Feel the points of contact with the earth and then tune into your soothing breathing rhythm. Allow the body to breath for you. Draw attention to your outbreath and listen to it closely, like a gently flowing breeze. Relax into each outbreath and give yourself permission to release daily concerns. Allow your mind to become fresh in this moment.

Inspiration and Aspirations:

Having taken some time to pause and soften, bring your attention to the space of your heart and ask yourself: "What is my heart's desire? What would make me truly happy?" Allow thoughts and ideas to bubble up, without needing to analyse them. Drop in another question, such as: "What do I wish for myself, my loved ones, and for the world?" or "What would it feel like to realise my heart's deepest desires?" Open your mind's awareness to see what comes up. Allow yourself to be optimistic, wishing the very best for yourself, as you would for your best friend. You may like to imagine this desire symbolically as an orb of white light at the heart, filling and expanding the heart, and then cascading throughout the whole body, saturating the mind with each out breath. As images of what you truly wish for come to mind, begin to see them actually happening, as you say to yourself on each out breath: "May I be truly happy". Breath-by-breath, imagine the fulfilment of your own dreams and aspirations blossoming, right here and right now.

Interdependence:

In the next stage of the practice, consider the truth of interdependence. You are inextricably dependent on many others to live your innermost dreams. Ask yourself now: "What would I love to receive from others, and from my environment, to realise my heart's desire?" With each in breath, say to yourself: "May I receive all I truly need, day-to-day, moment-to-moment". If it feels supportive for you, imagine all that you would love to receive coming into you in the form of white light on each in breath, filling your heart, and spreading through your entire body. Imagine here and now receiving all that you truly need and that reality is reaching up to support you.

Inner Transformation:

Next, explore what inner transformation may be needed to take you toward your intentions and aspirations. You need not only the blessings and assistance from others, but also to release some of your habit patterns that may be holding you back. Ask yourself: "What qualities of mind or behaviours do I wish to be free of?" or "What mental habits may be standing in the way of my deeper aspirations or blocking me from realising my true happiness?" As the answers come to mind, imagine these leaving you with each out breath, while saying to yourself: "May it be so". Imagine those transformations and releases happening within you right here and right now.

And now focus on any inner resources you would love to cultivate or strengthen in order to bring about your deepest happiness. What qualities of mind or heart would you love to be invested with? With each in breath, envision your own growth toward the realisation of your dreams. Once again, say to yourself: "May it be so". See yourself reshaping your inner world with these qualities strengthened and accessible within you. With each breath, imagine this transformation taking place within you, here and now.

Contributing to the World:

In the final stage of practice, you can explore your contribution to the world. To infuse your life with as much meaning as possible, reflect on what kind of mark you would like to make on the world. What is the greatest good that you can imagine bringing to the world so that it is a better place because you have been here? At the end of your life, imagine looking back with a deep sense of satisfaction, knowing this was a life well lived. With each out breath, imagine offering all the things that you would like to offer, drawing on your unique background, your talents, your interests, your training, your strengths, and your vision. Imagine offering these in the here and now. Imagine those around you receiving your offerings with joy and delight.

Closing the Practice:

To close the practice, release all images, and let ideas dissolve away. Let your awareness rest in utter simplicity and stillness, the place of emptiness. Rest in that sense of potential from which all your aspirations and intentions arise.

Moving Forward

*"Mindfulness is keeping your attention alive
in the present moment."*
~ Thich Nhat Hanh

A Spiralling Journey

The journey of both the social change activist, and the meditator, shifts and changes, moving in an ever-expanding spiral. To summarise the journey we've taken together through this book, I use a model developed by Rob Nairn, my first mindfulness teacher. Mindfulness, compassion, insight, and wisdom are like a spiral staircase, each supporting the next, and deepening the one before; capable of guiding a changemaker's approach to engagement.

Mindful Activism

To be mindful is to be awake in the present moment, while bringing interest and acceptance to what we find. Contemporary research has revealed the startling range of benefits that mindfulness brings to the individual, such as alleviating stress, sleeping better, and regulating our emotional reactivity. These are all important, but the real power of transforming our consciousness is the access it brings to a clear mind, an open heart, and wise action.

When we bring these qualities to activism, it allows a sense of curiosity and openness to the constant flow of change. It also implies accepting the present moment not by way of condoning harmful situations, but by evaluating clearly what actions need to be taken to allow transformation to take place.

Mindfulness alone can develop admirable qualities, yet without heartfulness - the ability to connect with the suffering of others - it can remain a self-centred technology that focuses more on personal growth, than community transformation. Some researchers have called this neo-liberal mindfulness, which falls short of the power of liberatory mindfulness.

Compassionate Activism

The second journey step gives us the capacity to see that many people are suffering, and resources us with the strength and commitment to try to alleviate it. Often, we are suffering too, and this is where self-compassion can become a life-enhancing practice.

Compassion differs from pity in that it recognises our interconnectedness and our equal status as human beings. We act, not from a place of superiority, but from knowing that our liberation is dependent on the liberation of all.

Compassion also differs from empathy in that we feel what others are feeling, but we do not get overwhelmed by those feelings, and we do not stop there. As we explored in the last chapter, empathy can lead to fatigue and burnout. Compassion has an action component, a wish to speak or act in a way that can offer support, and it is therefore linked to the well-being that we experience from helping others.

Insightful Activism

Bringing insight into your activism work means working to integrate your shadow tendencies. These are your mistakes and habits, which become companions along the path of growth. This is when moments of reflection allow us to course correct. Recognising our assumptions and judgements can be a painful process, but it is no reason to stop. It is only through our engagement with the people around us, who we perceive as difficult, that we can see our own character flaws. We may also begin to notice where we have been the beneficiaries of systems that privilege some, while oppressing others.

Insight also involves recognising certain truths, such as interdependence and impermanence; all things are connected and all things change. We often need to un-learn our conditioning and bias before we can re-learn in a way that makes us of greater benefit to others.

Wise Activism

This is where patience and resilience dwell. We may wish to achieve rapid results when we engage with issues of social or climate justice, but we need to keep in mind that if an unjust system took 200 years to put in place, it will likely take 200 years or more to dismantle.

We might lay the foundation in our own lifetime, but we will need to pass on the vision so that others can continue the work long after we are gone. Wise activism is the work of visionaries, those who have vast minds and can see what is possible, even when current circumstances suggest otherwise. We never know which of our actions will achieve results, so it is important to keep engaged. Our small daily actions can be carried out with a big, wholehearted intention.

Joyful Activism

When we link theories with practice, we experience the transformative power of praxis, through cycles of action, reflection and action. Our practice of mindfulness and compassion bears fruit when we engage with the world around us, which is why we do not need to wait until we are enlightened to be of service.

In fact, the act of service helps our path to enlightenment. As we have already explored, the final step in the journey of the compassionate activist is joyfulness, where we take great delight in moving beyond an ego-centric focus, in order to be of service to others.

Three Guiding Principles

One day, I was ranting on as usual about self-centred politicians who do not serve the needs of their communities. My husband asked me, "What would you do, if you were voted into power?" I was surprised at the clarity of my response and the simple answer to his impossible question:

1. Support people to find their calling.
2. Organise at the community level.
3. Expect disagreement and plan for it.

Purpose-based Education

If our education systems could focus on identifying and developing the natural talents and interests in children, we would all be happier and more sustained, while doing the work we love. Creativity expert, Ken Robinson was a great advocate for this approach, and most spiritual traditions agree that when we do what we love, in the service of others, we experience the deepest happiness.

I like to imagine the knock-on consequences of this at a community and societal level. Perhaps there would be less craving for material possessions and less focus on time as money. Maybe we could feel more satisfied with the simple delights of the natural world. With inner contentment, there would be less need for outward displays of status. The engine of consumerism would be starved of its power to make us buy more and more. Indeed, with a shift towards service, a fair income combined with the reward of working with others might be enough to satisfy our deeply human needs.

Self-organising Communities

We could organise service provision at the level of self-sustaining communities. These would only need to be between 150 and 200 people; small enough for everyone to know each other, but large enough to encompass a diverse range of skills and backgrounds.

The Climate Justice group that I am linked to in South Africa is proposing this same principle in terms of energy provision. The level of technology we currently have makes this possible, while still allowing us to operate at a size where everyone involved can know each other and hold each other accountable.

When I worked in Thailand, we experimented with running a non-hierarchical organisation in which everyone had access to all information and volunteers specialised in the projects where they had skills, as well as the ones that inspired them. We rotated the leadership to give people a chance to step up and step back at different times and different stages of the tsunami relief work.

Within our Expressive Movement dance community, we've also been exploring ways to engage with the harsh realities of the world around us and attempting to address how we can run agile organisations that do not exhaust their staff members. During COVID-19, we took part in an activation that demonstrated 'murmurations', in which birds flock, while keeping a safe distance. In these self-organising groups, there appears to be no leader, yet the entire gathering moves in harmony. In computer-generated animation, this is known as emergent behaviour, where individuals adhere to a set of simple rules:

- Separation: steer to avoid crowding, keep your own space, hold your own.
- Alignment: steer in the same average direction as the rest of the flock – not follow-your-leader but staying in connection with the birds flying closest to you and moving collectively.
- Cohesion: steer towards your flock mates, don't stray too far from the flock or you lose the safety-net of community.

We danced together, yet apart, at Constitution Hill, South Africa's symbol of democracy. From that embodied experience, we realised the possibility of changing the way communities and organisations work, opening space for collective emergent leadership. Within a network of trust, you can keep true to your own skills and interests. When the situation requires your specific set of skills, you may be called to lead, while others align. Then, as circumstances develop and change, you can step back as another steers the flock. Your community provides a safety net. Sometimes we guide; sometimes we support and follow, informed always by compassion and wisdom, intuition, and humility.

Welcome the Crack

With the direct democracy that is possible in small communities, there will inevitably be disagreements. We need to welcome this, and plan for it, with methods of skilful facilitation. As Leonard Cohen once wrote, "There is a crack in everything; that's how the light gets in." Conflict is not to be feared or avoided, but understood with compassion and curiosity, for it is usually in moments of disagreement or disruption that new insights and ideas emerge.

Many facilitation techniques are taught worldwide, but the ones I particularly love are constellation work and nonviolent communication. Constellation work derives from the techniques of African traditional healers for maintaining community cohesion. Through an embodied process of enactment, disagreements are explored and understood at a visceral level. With nonviolent communication, too, disagreements are explored from a place of personal responsibility, not blame or othering. Direct democracy requires an understanding of self, other, and the relationship between, in order to make decisions for the wider community.

While these three principles may be too simple and reflect my background in education and community work, I find myself returning to them again and again. I'd love to hear what three principles you would follow if you were asked to create a sustainable world.

In Closing

The call to stillness is a call to action. It is action from a deeply intuitive place of receptivity and compassion. Perhaps we are finally moving into the era of the sacred feminine, where we see humanity in connection with each other, mother earth, and all the more-than-human beings. The impulse of the sacred archetypal feminine is soft, yet strong; nurturing, yet fierce; and grounded by clear boundaries. When this works alongside the sacred masculine that is logical and protective, we can create a more harmonious world.

To grow into the compassionate activist that you already are, the primary work is that of purification, peeling away the layers of protection that have encased your heart. Once you are receptive and open, it's much easier to step forward in trust. Healing yourself, so that you project no harm onto others, is possibly the most powerful activism you can ever do.

I will close this book with the beautiful words of Nirmala Nair, a South African activist, who said:

"My challenge has thus been striking a balance between the inner and outer world - only possible when one is able to take a leap of faith. It was by no means an easy walk, there was no recipe waiting either. I look for signs and messages that confirm that my intuition and the external messages are aligned. I look for openings that come my way effortlessly. No more struggle. I am drawn to a new kind of work that unfolds spontaneously, effortlessly in co-evolution with nature. There is no winner and loser in this new kind of struggle. In this new kind of activism everyone has a role to play. Real diversity becomes the strength of all concerned in sustaining all life forms on this planet - not just warring humans.

An activist is like a dancer holding the tension of multiple strands, enveloping the constant unfolding, evolving with the dance of creation, and constantly expanding horizons. Consciously embracing the confusion, chaos, and beauty, loving, and living life in touch with hidden connections that are so elusive, yet so real. This for me is the Zen of an activist life."

A wonderful outcome of writing this book is that I have started to notice all the people around me who act compassionately in the world. They don't shout about it, or put it on social media, but they respond to the world, moment-by-moment, from an ethic of care.

I trust that what I have witnessed will be your discovery, too.

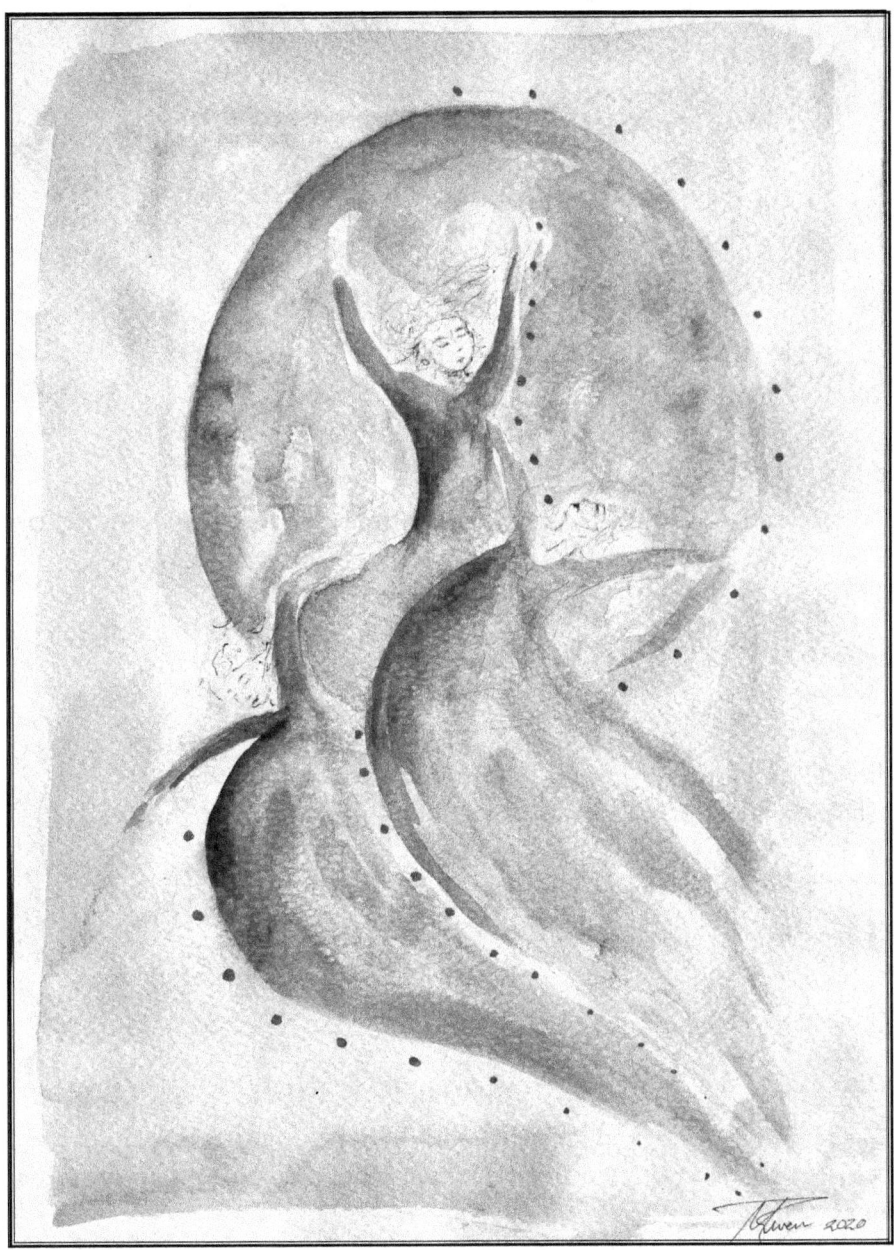

Pic 3. The Dance of Creation, by Maxine Puren

Appendices

Appendix A: Cultivating a Community of Trust and Inclusion Agreements for Multicultural Interactions

Created by © VISIONS

Try It On:

Be willing to "try on" new ideas or ways of doing things that might not be what you prefer or are familiar with.

Practice Self Focus:

Attend to, and speak about, your own experiences and responses. Do not speak for a whole group or express assumptions about the experience of others.

Understand the Difference Between Intent & Impact:

Try to understand and acknowledge impact. Denying the impact of something by focusing on intent is often more destructive than the initial interaction.

Practice "Both/And":

When speaking, substitute "and" for "but." This practice acknowledges and honours multiple realities.

Refrain From Blaming or Shaming Self & Others:

Practice giving skilful feedback.

Move Up/Move Back:

Encourage full participation by all present. Take note of who is speaking and who is not. If you tend to speak often, consider "moving back" and vice versa.

Practice Mindful Listening:

Try to avoid planning what you'll say as you listen to others. Be willing to be surprised, to learn something new. Listen with your whole self.

Confidentiality:

Take home learnings, but don't identify anyone other than yourself, now or later. If you want to follow up with anyone regarding something they said during a session, ask first and respect their wishes.

Right To Pass:

You can say "I pass" if you don't wish to speak.

http://www.eastbaymeditation.org

Appendix B: Universal Human Needs

Adapted from the work of Dr Marshall Rosenberg.

The needs below are grouped into three main categories (well-being, connection and self-experssion), and nine sub-categories of core human needs and values.

WELL-BEING

Sustenance	**Order**	**Safety**
balance	abundance	comfort
exercise, movement	calm, ease	peace
food, water, air	confidence	protection from harm
health	consistency	relaxation
nourishment	equanimity	security
nutrition	flow	shelter
rest	focus	trust
recreation	harmony	
rejuvenation	interdependence	
sleep	predictability	
touch	simplicity	
warmth	serenity	
wellness	stability	
vitality	structure	
energy	tranquillity	
	trust	
	wholeness	

CONNECTION

Love
affection, care
closeness
dignity
intimacy
equality
esteem
positive regard
generosity
kindness
mattering,
importance
nurturing
support, help
respect, honouring
valuing, prizing

Empathy
awareness
acceptance
acknowledgment
communication
compassion
consideration
empathy
openness
presence
recognition
receptivity
sensitivity
understanding

Belonging
collaboration
team
community
companionship
cooperation
fellowship
generosity
inclusion
home
hospitality
welcoming
mutuality
reciprocity
partnership

SELF-EXPRESSION

Meaning
achievement
success
aliveness
appreciation
gratitude
beauty
celebration
mourning
contribution
discovery
efficacy, effectiveness
excellence
mastery, skill
inspiration
learning
passion, purpose
vision
wisdom
wonder

Freedom
adventure
actualisation
autonomy
choice
creativity, innovation
growth, challenge
humour
independence
joy
play
fun
spontaneity

Honesty
authenticity
clarity
congruence
dependability
integrity
power
empowerment
presence
reliability
trust

FEELINGS

Feelings are bodily felt experiences and emotions that tell us whether our needs are being met or not met. They also provide useful information about what we are observing, thinking, and wanting.

When our needs **are being met**, we feel:

PEACEFUL
tranquil calm
content
engrossed
absorbed
expansive
serene
blissful
satisfied
relaxed
relieved
quiet
carefree
composed
fulfilled

LOVING
warm
affectionate
tender
appreciative
friendly
sensitive
compassionate
grateful
nurtured
amorous
trusting
open
thankful
radiant
adoring
passionate

GLAD
happy
excited
hopeful
joyful
satisfied
delighted
encouraged
grateful
confident
inspired
touched
proud
exhilarated
ecstatic
optimistic
glorious

PLAYFUL
energetic
effervescent
invigorated
zestful
refreshed
impish
alive, lively
exuberant
giddy
adventurous
mischievous
jubilant
goofy
buoyant
electrified

INTERESTED
involved
inquisitive
intense
enriched
absorbed
alert
aroused
astonished
concerned
curious
eager
enthusiastic
fascinated
intrigued
surprised
helpful

When our needs **are not being met**, we feel:

ANGRY
impatient
pessimistic
disgruntled
frustrated
irritable
edgy
grouchy
agitated
exasperated
disgusted
irked
cantankerous
animosity
bitter
rancorous
irate
furious
angry
hostile
enraged
violent

SAD
lonely
heavy
troubled
helpless
gloomy
overwhelmed
distant
despondent
discouraged
distressed
dismayed
disheartened
despairing
sorrowful
unhappy

depressed
blue
miserable
dejected
melancholy

SCARED
afraid
fearful
terrified
startled
nervous
jittery
horrified
anxious
worried
anguished
lonely
insecure
sensitive
shocked
apprehensive
dread
jealous
desperate
suspicious
frightened

TIRED
exhausted
fatigued
inert
lethargic
indifferent
weary
overwhelmed
fidgety
helpless
heavy

sleepy
disinterested
reluctant
passive
dull
bored
listless
blah, meh
mopey
comatose

CONFUSED
frustrated
perplexed
hesitant
troubled
uncomfortable
withdrawn
apathetic
embarrassed
hurt
uneasy
irritated
suspicious
unsteady
puzzled
restless
boggled
chagrined
unglued
detached
sceptical

Acknowledgements

This book is the work of an entire community and while I can't thank everyone individually, there are certain groups I feel honoured to mention. Two of my passions - compassionate mindfulness and social justice – had been living separate lives. The idea to bring them together germinated in the listening presence of friend and coach, Felicity Joan Hart and during walks through the park with dharma sister Jane Burt. In 2019, I decided to offer this intersection as a course called the Activists' Way. Each week, as I prepared the material, the words for this book emerged. I recorded the sessions and transcribed, combining the ideas from each group with my own experience and insights. These friends have continued to be involved as cheerleaders, and many have played a direct role in the midwifery of this book: Andrea Rolfes, Ann Simmonds, Anni Snyman, Ayesha Osman, Boitumelo Mokoena, Chantal Nativel, Charlotte Johnson, Cynthia Stimpel, Dirk de Waal, Dorothy Brislin, Ela Manga, Hector Kunene, Kai Crooks-Chissano, June Bellamy, Marj Murray, Nan Lutz, Stacey Rozen, Lindi Bell, Nereida Ripero-Muniz, Rizwana Osman, Simon Sizwe Mayson, Tara Polzer Ngwato and Zelda Barker – a community of healers, educators, artists, activists, whistleblowers, researchers, yoga teachers and mindfulness trainers.

Once the first draft was complete, I tentatively shared with trusted readers, Rob Nairn, Lin Cassidy, Kerri Martinaglia, Joanne Crossley, Steven Heyman and Robyn Sheldon. They nudged me to include more stories, reminding me that through the personal we understand the political. Each cycle produced edits and changes. Then we were all forced into lockdown and it felt strange that the most activist thing I could do was to stay at home! It helped me re-evaluate the strong desire to engage, and to recognize that the challenges in our world are symptoms of our untamed minds, not the causes. During this quiet time, alternative forms of activism became clear, such as the gentle practices of art, poetry and performance. I ran two more courses online with willing collaborators from further afield: Candice Tootell, Ella Dessington, Emma Mills, Evelyn Roe, Isabel Mullery, Kate Ballenden, Lin Cassidy, Lyn Lupke, Sarah Foale and Shayna de Kock. Then it was time to look for editors and publishers. Again, the local community offered everything I needed – Robyn Porteus and Natasha Fracchiolla from Room206, Ela Manga and Marj Murray from Portal Works, and Rutendo Ngara, healer and engineer. This long gestated book was finally birthed with these midwives at hand.

I would also like to thank the Heart-Mind yogis, ever present to offer insights into Jo'burg life, the academy and the world itself. The push back against injustice is deeply imprinted in their bones and bodies, as well as the healing power of their art: Andrea Rolfes, Carina Comrie, Carolyn Carew, Hayley Gewer, Levinia Jones, Lisa Jaffe, Mehita Iqani, Nicky Falkof, Roshan Dadoo, Sarah Steele, Yavini Naidoo, Zana Marovic, and from across the oceans, Ondine Hogeboom.

Writing out these names makes me realize that I have been held in a powerful circle of women, from as far back as university days with Claudia Harrison and Melanie Gilbert. I'm also lucky to have walked beside wonderful men who have offered me great encouragement over the years: Rob Nairn, Donal Creedon, Charlie Morley, Bodhi Garrett, Andy Taylor and Warren Nebe.

My family, too, has given me the freedom to live away from the UK for most of my adult life. Thank you to Jane, Peter and Richard Dixon-Clarke, and to my sisters-in-law, Jenny and Clare, my nieces Tegen, Poppy and Emily, and my nephew, Billy. May you inherit a world filled with compassion and wisdom. My newer family, the Draper clan, welcomed me so warmly to South Africa that I will be forever grateful.

Finally, my deepest thanks go to the one who sits beside me every morning and lies beside me at night, the one who is as compassionate as they come, my beloved husband, Mike Draper.

References

Introduction

Barks, C., Rumi, J.A.D., Nicholson, R.A., Arberry, A.J. and Moyne, J., 2006. A year with Rumi: Daily readings. HarperSanFrancisco.

Chenoweth, E., Stephan, M.J. and Stephan, M., 2011. Why civil resistance works: The strategic logic of nonviolent conflict. Columbia University Press.

Dixon-Clarke, L.J., Garrett, B. and NATR team. 2005. From Disaster to Development. https://www.andamannetwork.org/wp-content/uploads/2020/07/disaster_to_development.pdf

Eze, M.O., 2010. Ubuntu: Toward a new public discourse. In Intellectual History in Contemporary South Africa (pp. 181-192). Palgrave Macmillan, New York.

Gilbert, P. ed., 2017. Compassion: Concepts, research and applications. Taylor & Francis.

Jones, V., 2018. Beyond the messy truth: How we came apart, how we come together. Ballantine Books.

Chapter 1

Adriansen, H.K. and Knudsen, H., 2013. Two ways to support reflexivity: Teaching managers to fulfil an undefined role: 'A problem cannot be solved at the same level of thinking that created it'—Albert Einstein. Teaching Public Administration, 31(1), pp.108-123.

Allen, S., 2018. The science of gratitude. Conshohocken, PA: John Templeton Foundation.

Cameron, J., 2020. The artist's way. Lev..

Dana, D., 2018. The Polyvagal theory in therapy: engaging the rhythm of regulation (Norton series on interpersonal neurobiology). WW Norton & Company.

Draper-Clarke, Lucy; de Beer, Welma (2022): Our HAPPy Place - Healing Arts for Trauma Integration. figshare. Media. https://doi.org/10.6084/m9.figshare.19630017.v3

Hanson, R., 2016. Hardwiring happiness: The new brain science of contentment, calm, and confidence. Harmony.

Harvey, A., 2005. Sacred activism. Hartley Film Foundation.

Irwin, E. (1999) Healing Relaxation, London: Rider.

King Jr, L., 1968. "I've Been to the Mountaintop" by Dr. Martin Luther King, Jr.

Lambert, K.G., 2003. The life and career of Paul MacLean: A journey toward neurobiological and social harmony. Physiology & behavior, 79(3), pp.343-349.

Lhamo, N., 2014. Sowa Rigpa: An Avenue for Personal Health and Well-being.

Morley, C., 2021. Dreaming Through Darkness: Shine Light into the Shadow to Live the Life of Your Dreams. Hay House, Inc.

Porges, S.W., 2017. The pocket guide to the polyvagal theory: The transformative power of feeling safe. WW Norton & Co.

Roth, G., 2011. Maps to ecstasy: The healing power of movement. New World Library.

Von Holdt, K., Langa, M., Molapo, S., Mogapi, N., Ngubeni, K., Dlamini, J. and Kirsten, A., 2011. Insurgent citizenship, collective violence and the struggle for a place in the New South Africa. Centre for the Study of Violence and Reconciliation, University of the Witwatersrand. Accessed June, 2, p.2015.

Williamson, M., 2008. "Our Deepest Fear" poem. A Return to Love: Reflections on the Principles of "A Course in Miracles"

Chapter 2

Buck, P. S. (1954). My several worlds: A personal record. Cutchogue, NY: Buccaneer Books.

Kohlberg, L., 1971. Stages of moral development. Moral education, 1(51), pp.23-92.

Lawler, K.A., Younger, J.W., Piferi, R.L., Jobe, R.L., Edmondson, K.A. and Jones, W.H., 2005. The unique effects of forgiveness on health: An exploration of pathways. Journal of behavioral medicine, 28(2), pp.157-167.

Mindfulness Assoc. (2011). Mindfulness Based Living Course, p.38

Nairn, R., 2001. Diamond mind: A psychology of meditation. Shambhala Publications.

Wallace, B.A. and Shapiro, S.L., 2006. Mental balance and well-being: building bridges between Buddhism and Western psychology. American Psychologist, 61(7), p.690.

Chapter 3

Corbett, Sarah., https://www.ted.com/talks/sarah_corbett_activism_needs_introverts

Dahl, C.J., Lutz, A. and Davidson, R.J., 2015. Reconstructing and deconstructing the self: cognitive mechanisms in meditation practice. Trends in cognitive sciences, 19(9), pp.515-523.

Hanh, T.N., 2016. The miracle of mindfulness, gift edition: An introduction to the practice of meditation. Beacon Press.
Iyer, Deepa., https://buildingmovement.org/
Lau, Evelyn., Dec 26, 2021. https://www.thenationalnews.com/arts-culture/books/2021/12/26/a-look-back-at-desmond-tutus-greatest-quotes-from-kindness-to-forgiveness/
Palmer, Sian., 9 May 2020 Ancestors and Movement. https://youtu.be/Dc1ge6zl77g
Ricard, M., 2013. On the path to enlightenment: Heart advice from the great Tibetan masters. Shambhala Publications.
Rosenberg, M.B., 2002. Nonviolent communication: A language of compassion. Encinitas, CA: Puddledancer press.
Rozen, Stacey., https://www.ted.com/talks/stacey_rozen_a_craftivist_s_ode_to_the_face_mask

Chapter 4
Dogen, Z.M., 1985. Moon in a dewdrop: Writings of Zen master Dogen. Macmillan.
Hanh, T.N., 2008. Understanding our mind. ReadHowYouWant. com.
Hooks, B., 2014. Teaching to transgress. Routledge.
Krishnamurti, J. and Bohm, D., 1999. The limits of thought: discussions. Psychology Press.
Kornfield, J., 1993. The Buddhist path and social responsibility. ReVision, 16(2), pp.83-86.
Nairn, R. and Regan-Addis, H., 2019. From Mindfulness to Insight: Meditations to Release Your Habitual Thinking and Activate Your Inherent Wisdom. Shambhala Publications.
Suzuki, S., 2020. Zen mind, beginner's mind. Shambhala Publications.
Tillich, P., 1954. Love, power, and justice: Ontological analyses and ethical applications (Vol. 38). Oxford University Press, USA.
Trungpa, C., 2001. Great eastern sun: The wisdom of Shambhala. Shambhala Publications.
Varela, F.J., Thompson, E. and Rosch, E., 2017. The embodied mind, revised edition: Cognitive science and human experience. MIT press.

Chapter 5
Balkenhol, M., 2016. Silence and the politics of compassion. Commemorating slavery in the Netherlands. Social Anthropology/Anthropologie Sociale, 24(3), pp.278-293.
Chang, D.F. and Berk, A., 2009. Making cross-racial therapy work: A phenomenological study of clients' experiences of cross-racial therapy. Journal of counseling psychology, 56(4), p.521.
Chinyowa, K, in Barnes, H., Carter, C.B. and Nebe, W. eds., 2022. Innovative Methods for Applied Drama and Theatre Practice in African Contexts: Drama for Life. Cambridge Scholars Publishing.

Chödrön, P., 2017. The compassion book: Teachings for awakening the heart. Shambhala Publications.
Carruthers, C., 2018. Unapologetic: A Black, queer, and feminist mandate for radical movements. Beacon Press.
DiAngelo, R., 2018. White fragility: Why it's so hard for white people to talk about racism. Beacon Press.
Falkof, N., 2021. Worrier state: Risk, anxiety and moral panic in South Africa. In Worrier state. Manchester University Press.
Gorski, P.C., 2019. Fighting racism, battling burnout: Causes of activist burnout in US racial justice activists. Ethnic and Racial Studies, 42(5), pp.667-687.
King, R. 2018. Mindful of race: Transforming racism from the inside out. Sounds True.
van Dernoot Lipsky, L., 2010. Trauma stewardship: An everyday guide to caring for self while caring for others. ReadHowYouWant. com.
Lorde, A., 2017. A burst of light: And other essays. Courier Dover Publications.
Magee, R.V., 2021. The inner work of racial justice: Healing ourselves and transforming our communities through mindfulness. Penguin.
Menakem, R. 2021) My grandmother's hands: Racialized trauma and the pathway to mending our hearts and bodies. Penguin UK.
Mindfulness Assoc. (2015) Compassion Based Living Course
Morinis, A. 2007. Everyday holiness: The Jewish spiritual path of mussar. Boston, MA: Trumpeter Books.
Nair, N., 2004. On 'being'and 'becoming'… the many faces of an activist. Agenda, 18(60), pp.28-32.
Powell, J.A. and Toppin Jr, E., 2021. Uprooting authoritarianism: Deconstructing the stories behind narrow identities and building a society of belonging. Colum. J. Race & L., 11, p.1.
Smith, D. T., in Murphy, Colleen, 20 Sept 2021, What is White Savior Complex and Why is it Harmful. https://www.health.com/mind-body/health-diversity-inclusion/white-savior-complex
Tanur, C., 2015. The inner work of organisations. MA Dissertation

Chapter 6
Bokar Rinpoche., 1999. Tara The Feminine Divine.
Castaneda, C., 2009. The Wheel Of Time: The Shamans Of Mexico Their Thoughts About Life De. Simon and Schuster.
Hanh, T.N., 2002. Present moment wonderful moment: Mindfulness verses for daily living. Parallax Press.
Macy, J. and Johnstone, C., 2012. Active hope: How to face the mess we're in without going crazy. New World Library.
Pádraig Ó Tuama and Marilyn Nelson., October 28, 2021. "So let us pick up the stones over which we stumble, friends, and build altars." https://onbeing.org/programs/padraig-o-tuama-and-marilyn-nelson-so-let-us-pick-up-the-stones-over-which-we-stumble-friends-and-build-altars-/#transcript

Chapter 7
Armstrong, K., 2011. Twelve steps to a compassionate life. Random House.
Chödrön, P., 2001. Start where you are: A guide to compassionate living. Shambhala Publications.
Dunn, Elizabeth,. 2019. Helping others makes us happier – but it matters how we do it. https://www.ted.com/talks/elizabeth_dunn_helping_others_makes_us_happier_but_it_matters_how_we_do_it
Harvey, A., 2005. Sacred activism. Hartley Film Foundation.
Lama, D. and Novick, R.M., 2002. Illuminating the path to enlightenment. Thubten Dhargye Ling, Long beach.
Shantideva. 2007. The Way of the Bodhisattva. Shambhala Publications.
Wallace, B.A., 2010. The The Four Immeasurables: Practices to Open the Heart.
Watson, Lilla,. https://en.wikipedia.org/wiki/Lilla_Watson#cite_note-3. 8 June 2022

Chapter 8
Freedman, R., 1998. Martha Graham: A dancer's life. Houghton Mifflin Harcourt.
García, H. and Miralles, F., 2017. Ikigai: The Japanese secret to a long and happy life. Penguin.
Kang, Y., Strecher, V.J., Kim, E. and Falk, E.B., 2019. Purpose in life and conflict-related neural responses during health decision-making. Health Psychology, 38(6), p.545.
Kimmerer, R., 2013. Braiding sweetgrass: Indigenous wisdom, scientific knowledge and the teachings of plants. Milkweed editions.
McNaughton, W & Martin, C.E.,A Responsibility to Light. https://www.themarginalian.org/2017/05/15/focus-wendy-macnaughton-courtney-martin-poster/
Ogyen.Trinley Dorje (17th Karmapa) and Derris, K., 2014. The heart is noble: changing the world from the inside out. Shambhala Publications.

Chapter 9
Hanh, T.N., 2008. Breathe, You Are Alive!: The Sutra on the Full Awareness of Breathing: Easyread Super Large 24pt Edition. ReadHowYouWant. com.
Huffington, A., 2014. Thrive: The third metric to redefining success and creating a life of well-being, wisdom, and wonder. Harmony.
Kimmerer, R., 2013. Braiding sweetgrass: Indigenous wisdom, scientific knowledge and the teachings of plants. Milkweed editions.
Kok, B.E. and Singer, T., 2017. Effects of contemplative dyads on engagement and perceived social connectedness over 9 months of mental training: A randomized clinical trial. Jama psychiatry, 74(2), pp.126-134.
Ncube, N., 2006. The tree of life project. International Journal of Narrative Therapy & Community Work, 2006(1), pp.3-16.
Solnit, R., 2016. Hope in the dark: Untold histories, wild possibilities. Haymarket Books.
Tonn, B.E. and Ogle, E., 2002. A vision for communities in the 21st century: back to the future. Futures, 34(8), pp.717-734.

Chapter 10
Blake, W., 1977. The Portable William Blake. Penguin.
Claiborne, S., Wilson-Hartgrove, J. and Okoro, E., 2010. Common prayer: A liturgy for ordinary radicals. Zondervan.
Gibran, K. and Bushrui, S.B., 2012. The prophet: A new annotated edition. Simon and Schuster.
Kok, B.E., Coffey, K.A., Cohn, M.A., Catalino, L.I., Vacharkulksemsuk, T., Algoe, S.B., Brantley, M. and Fredrickson, B.L., 2013. How positive emotions build physical health: Perceived positive social connections account for the upward spiral between positive emotions and vagal tone. Psychological science, 24(7), pp.1123-1132.
Lama, D., Tutu, D. and Abrams, D.C., 2016. The book of joy: Lasting happiness in a changing world. Penguin.
Powers, S., 2008. Insight Yoga: An innovative synthesis of traditional yoga, meditation, and Eastern approaches to healing and well-being. Shambhala Publications.
Ricard, M., 2015. Altruism: The power of compassion to change yourself and the world. Little, Brown.
Singer, T. and Bolz, M., 2013. Compassion: Bridging practice and science. Max Planck Institute for Human Cognitive and Brain Sciences.
Solnit, R., 2016. Hope in the dark: Untold histories, wild possibilities. Haymarket Books.
Tutu, D., Tutu, M.A., Kae-Kazim, H. and Badaki, Y., 2014. The book of forgiving: The fourfold path for healing ourselves and our world. San Francisco: HarperOne.
Wallace, B.A., 2010. The The Four Immeasurables: Practices to Open the Heart.

Moving Forward
Bishop, S.R., Lau, M., Shapiro, S., Carlson, L., Anderson, N.D., Carmody, J., Segal, Z.V., Abbey, S., Speca, M., Velting, D. and Devins, G., 2004. Mindfulness: A proposed operational definition. Clinical psychology: Science and practice, 11(3), p.230.
Draper-Clarke, Lucy; O'Hagan, Thandi (2022): #MarketMurmurations. figshare. Media. https://doi.org/10.6084/m9.figshare.19706890.v2
Nair, N., 2004. On 'being' and 'becoming'... the many faces of an activist. Agenda, 18(60), pp.28-32.
Tonn, B.E. and Ogle, E., 2002. A vision for communities in the 21st century: back to the future. Futures, 34(8), pp.717-734.

Appendices
Center for Nonviolent Communication, 2005, Feelings and Needs Inventory, www.cnvc.org
EBMC, March 4, 2022, Agreements for Multicultural Interactions, https://eastbaymeditation.org/2022/03/agreements-for-multicultural-interactions/

About the Author

Dr Lucy Draper-Clarke is an educator, mindfulness mentor, and researcher-practitioner at the University of the Witwatersrand (Wits) in Johannesburg, South Africa. After graduating from Oxford University in 1989, she obtained a PGCE and moved to Botswana to work in education. She taught in schools, wrote textbooks and later ran an educational publishing company, consulting to the United Nations.

In 2005, Lucy helped set up the North Andaman Tsunami Relief in Thailand and worked on disaster relief and educational initiatives. On her return to Botswana, she became Deputy Principal at Maru-a-Pula school, while also training as a yoga teacher and mindfulness facilitator.

She moved to South Africa in 2010 to study at Wits, where she was awarded a doctorate in Mindfulness, through the School of Education. Her current focus on Compassionate Activism offers human service professionals and activists the skills they need to prevent burnout, increase resilience, and cultivate wise action.

Lucy is a postgraduate supervisor and research associate at Drama for Life, a department dedicated to social transformation and healing. She has a particular interest in studying the African Wisdom Traditions that have supported communities for generations.

She has taken refuge both in the Karma Kagyu School of Buddhism, and the Zen lineage of Thich Nhat Hanh, and attends regular retreats to deepen her own meditation practice. Building on what she has learned, she loves to facilitate courses and retreats around Southern Africa.

Nothing gives her more joy than sharing life-enhancing, movement and sitting practices so that everyone can discover their own creative and purposeful lives.

www.ingramcontent.com/pod-product-compliance
Lightning Source LLC
Chambersburg PA
CBHW072002290426
44109CB00018B/2104